PHOTOSHOP
ON THE iPad

CREATIVITY ON THE GO

ROB DE WINTER

Photoshop on the iPad
Rob de Winter

English language edition © 2023 by Pearson Education. All Rights Reserved.
Authorized translation of *Photoshop op de iPad* (ISBN 978-94-6356-2003) by Rob de Winter, published by Van Duuren Media B.V. ©2021 Van Duuren Media B.V. All rights reserved.

New Riders
www.peachpit.com
Peachpit Press is an imprint of Pearson Education, Inc.
To report errors, please send a note to errata@peachpit.com

Notice of Rights

Notice of Liability

Trademarks

Executive Editor: Laura Norman
Development Editor: Linda Laflamme
Senior Production Editor: Tracey Croom
Tech Editor: Conrad Chavez
Compositor: Rob de Winter
Proofreader: Kim Wimpsett
Indexer: James Minkin
Cover Design: Rob de Winter with Chuti Prasertsith
Interior Design: Rob de Winter

ISBN-13:   978-0-13-808471-4
ISBN-10:   0-13-808471-8

4 2023

Where are the exercise files?

You must register your purchase on **peachpit.com** in order to access the bonus content. After that, you can copy the exercise files to your *Creative Cloud Files* and easily open these files in Photoshop on the iPad.

TIP: If Photoshop on the iPad or Adobe Creative Cloud is completely new to you, you may want to first read Chapter 1 and the beginning of Chapter 2 (until we open the first file on page 18). If you already have a Creative Cloud account (free or paid), you can immediately follow the steps below.

1. Go to **www.peachpit.com/psipad**.
2. Sign in or create a new account.
3. Click *Submit* (**Figure 0.1**).

Figure 0.1 Register your book.

4. Click the *Access Bonus Content* link below the Photoshop on the iPad title on the My Registered Products tab on your Account page (**Figure 0.2**).

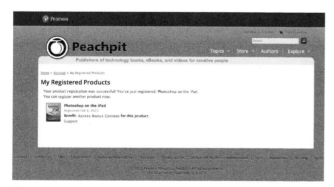

Figure 0.2 Access your bonus content after the book appears on the My Registered Products page.

Option 1: Copy to Files

On the My Registered Products page, you'll find a link to a shared Creative Cloud Files folder. That's the easiest way to copy the entire exercise folder automatically to your Creative Cloud Files at once. You can open this page on your iPad or desktop.

1. Click the link to the shared Creative Cloud Files folder.
2. You're now on the Creative Cloud website where the exercise files are located. Click the *Copy to Files* button (**Figure 0.3**).

Figure 0.3 Copy to Files.

3. If you're not yet logged in with your Creative Cloud account, do that now. Log in with the Adobe ID you also use to log into Photoshop on the iPad.

The files are now automatically copied to your Creative Cloud Files folder. Syncing may take a few seconds. After that, you can find them here:

ON THE IPAD: Before you can access the files on your iPad, you must first download the *Adobe Creative Cloud app* from the Apple App Store (more on that in Chapter 1). When you open the Creative Cloud app and log in with your Adobe ID, your Creative Cloud files are automatically available in the *Files app* on your iPad. When you open or import a file into Photoshop on the iPad, navigate to the *Creative Cloud* folder and then navigate to the *Photoshop on the iPad Exercise Files folder* (**Figure 0.4**). This is the folder you copied in the previous steps.

ON THE DESKTOP: Make sure you have the Creative Cloud application installed on your desktop computer as well. You can then find the files in the left bar of

Explorer (Windows) or Finder (macOS). Don't see that folder? Then you can also access the folder through the Creative Cloud app. Open the Creative Cloud app and navigate to the Files tab. Then click Open Sync folder in the left bar (**Figure 0.5**). The Creative Cloud Files folder will now open. The Photoshop on iPad exercise files can be found there.

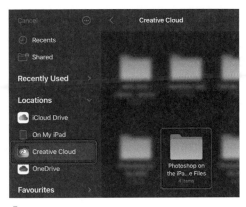

Figure 0.4 Exercise files on your iPad

Figure 0.5 Exercise files on your computer

Option 2: Other ways to copy files

If for some reason the exercise files cannot be synced through Creative Cloud Files, you can also download a ZIP file from the My Registered Products tab by clicking the Access Bonus Content link. In this case, your options include:

EXTERNAL HARD DRIVE: Download the ZIP file containing the exercise files onto your desktop computer, unzip it and copy the files to an external hard drive. Connect the hard drive to the iPad, and copy the files to your iPad using the *Files app*.

CLOUD STORAGE: If you use another cloud storage service, such as OneDrive, Dropbox or Google Drive, you can also copy the extracted ZIP file containing the exercise files there. On your iPad, download your storage service's app from the App Store. When you open the app and log in, your files are immediately available in the *Files app* and in other apps, such as Photoshop. You can read more about ways to put files or photos on your iPad in Chapter 1.

NOTE: The media files provided with this book are practice files, provided for your personal, educational use in these lessons only. You are not authorized to use these files commercially or to publish, share, or distribute them in any form without written permission from the individual copyright holders of the various items. Do not share projects created with these lesson files publicly. This includes, but is not limited to, distribution via social media or online video platforms such as YouTube and Vimeo. You will find a complete copyright statement on the copyright page at the beginning of this book.

Pearson's Commitment to Diversity, Equity, and Inclusion

Pearson is dedicated to creating bias-free content that reflects the diversity of all learners. We embrace the many dimensions of diversity, including but not limited to race, ethnicity, gender, socioeconomic status, ability, age, sexual orientation, and religious or political beliefs.

Education is a powerful force for equity and change in our world. It has the potential to deliver opportunities that improve lives and enable economic mobility. As we work with authors to create content for every product and service, we acknowledge our responsibility to demonstrate inclusivity and incorporate diverse scholarship so that everyone can achieve their potential through learning. As the world's leading learning company, we have a duty to help drive change and live up to our purpose to help more people create a better life for themselves and to create a better world.

Our ambition is to purposefully contribute to a world where:

» Everyone has an equitable and lifelong opportunity to succeed through learning.
» Our educational products and services are inclusive and represent the rich diversity of learners.
» Our educational content accurately reflects the histories and experiences of the learners we serve.
» Our educational content prompts deeper discussions with learners and motivates them to expand their own learning (and worldview).

While we work hard to present unbiased content, we want to hear from you about any concerns or needs with this Pearson product so that we can investigate and address them.

» Please contact us with concerns about any potential bias at **www.pearson.com/report-bias.html**.

Special thanks

That this book is in front of you now is at least 50% because I was lucky enough to meet the right people at the right time, because of the love of family and friends and because of the people who gave me all kinds of opportunities along the way in life. In no particular order, and knowing that I cannot name everyone, my great thanks go to these people:

All interviewees who contributed to this book: Ted Chin, Russell Brown, Frankie Cihi and Magdiel Lopez. Thanks for sharing your knowledge and beautiful images. It was truly inspiring to work with you.

The Adobe Photoshop team, especially Ryan Dumlao. Thanks for your enthusiasm about this book, for writing the foreword and for your help in answering questions.

The kind, committed people at Pearson, including Laura Norman and Tracey Croom for making this project possible and Linda Laflamme and Conrad Chavez for the great tips and positive guidance.

Bob van Duuren, Wouter Vermeulen and all the other amazing people at my Dutch publisher Van Duuren Media. It all started with you!

Ivan for your patience, love and great care!

Mom and Dad for your enthusiasm, love and opportunities I got thanks to you.

Peter Wirmusky for all the English tips and tricks and fun conversations.

Bart Van de Wiele for your help and motivating conversations when we were both writing and translating our books.

Edwin van Laar for your critical eye, feedback and the many years of friendship.

Hilde Maassen, Arie van Tilborg, Karin Donk and Sanne Plaisier for the opportunities and friendship at and outside Grafisch Lyceum Rotterdam.

All the dear family and friends who are a very important part of my life. It's impossible to name everyone, but you know who I mean ;-)

Contents

Chapter 3
Ted Chin   34

Chapter 4
Photo composition   44

Chapter 5
Russell Brown

Chapter 6
Retouching

Chapter 7
Frankie Cihi

Foreword by Ryan Dumlao

Photoshop has been my constant companion in life. I picked up Photoshop 4.0 as a kid, and it's been with me through every passion, interest and journey that life has given me. I used it to create graphics for my Pokémon website during the dot-com boom, design textures for computer games in high school, and needlessly polish covers and diagrams for my assignments in undergrad. As I studied optics and photonics at UCLA, I explored photography along the way—and Photoshop showed me yet another powerful corner of the infinite digital world it's helped to build. Its reach and value to everything I want to do are vast and endless. This journey finally culminated when I was able to join the Photoshop team as a product manager a few years ago, looking to bring a proper version of Photoshop into the mobile world.

We launched Photoshop on the iPad in 2019 knowing the huge challenge still ahead of us to keep building, improving and growing this amazing tool to a powerful app for everyone. We wanted to harness the power of the touchscreen and Apple Pencil, as well as bring the ability to create just about anywhere— in the office, on the couch, riding a train, and anywhere out in the world. My experience has taught me that using Photoshop means 100 different things to 100 different people, and our mission is to meet all those needs. We always listen first to people like you, discovering what it means to use Photoshop in the 21st century and will continue to do so for years to come.

Rob de Winter has done a tremendous job of capturing the versatility, power and possibility that Photoshop on the iPad espouses with this book. He's been deeply connected to the Photoshop community for years, and we were delighted to have him teach workshops on Photoshop on the iPad at Adobe MAX 2020 through 2022. There's a lot to learn and re-learn for people wanting to do complex composites and photo retouching on the iPad, and Rob's curriculum has guided thousands in learning to do so.

It was only natural after MAX that he put pen to paper and draw up this fantastic manual on Photoshop on the iPad. True to form, Rob informed this guide through interviews from some of the Photoshop team's favorite artists. Ted Chin has been a longtime collaborator since back when Photoshop on the iPad was a small project codenamed "Rocket." Frankie Cihi is an amazing artist and strong advocate for Photoshop on the iPad from Tokyo, my favorite city in the world. Magdiel Lopez helped me celebrate Photoshop's 30th birthday when we hosted Adobe Live! together, creating captivating digital posters on the fly. I'm pleased they were able to help contribute and offer their wisdom to you all. It's been a great privilege to get to know so many creative, smart and passionate people. But most of all, through Rob's expertise and excellent teaching style, I hope many more of you will follow in their footsteps. I know that this book will remain a gold-standard guide to mastering the product we all hold so dear, and I hope you enjoy it.

Ryan Dumlao
Product Manager for Photoshop on the iPad

Introduction

WHO IS THIS BOOK FOR?

Creativity on the go. That's the subtitle of this book and the fantastic mobile power we now have. Now that Photoshop, Lightroom, Illustrator and Fresco have been made iPad compatible, you can get creative on the go or in a studio in a very intuitive and mobile way. But even when you're not on the road, Photoshop on the iPad is a great addition! At your workplace, but also on your couch or in your garden. In this book you'll see how to combine Photoshop with other applications, and you'll learn how to select, mask, retouch and create photo compositions, social media images and much more in Photoshop on the iPad. I wish you lots of fun with this book!

Photoshop on the iPad

Photoshop on an iPad. It once began as a joke within the Photoshop team: "Let's try to make Photoshop run on an iPad." That joke turned out to be a hit. Since then, the iPad version has grown into a promising and serious project, and the app has a prominent place within Adobe's Creative Cloud ecosystem.

The project did take some doing. Copying Photoshop one to one to an iPad was not an option. To make such an extensive program work well on a touchscreen, the entire interface had to be redesigned. More compact because of the smaller screen, but with larger buttons so it could be operated with fingers or an Apple Pencil. A touchscreen requires very different controls than a regular PC or Mac.

In the end, an approach was taken where Photoshop on the iPad runs entirely on the original code of the desktop version of Photoshop. The interface has been modified, and the most important and the most frequently used Photoshop functions have been added one by one.

© Ted Chin

© Magdiel Lopez

Don't expect every desktop feature to be present in Photoshop on the iPad. That means that sometimes you'll have to search a bit for an alternative tool or method. I honestly don't think that's a bad thing. In a way, it's even refreshing, because you'll look at the app in a different way. For specific, advanced functions, you'll sometimes have to switch to the desktop. With cloud syncing, switching between devices is fast and easy.

Creating photo compositions, selecting, masking, retouching and painting are very intuitive on the iPad. The touchscreen combined with this custom Photoshop interface sometimes feels like you're modeling. And, on top of that, the combination with mobile apps like Lightroom, Fresco and Illustrator turns your iPad into a fantastic graphics workstation.

Purpose of this book

My goal in writing this book is to inspire you, the reader. I had the same idea with my previous Dutch-language book *Photoshop Masters*, where I interviewed six well-known Photoshop artists. I combined those interviews with fun tutorials so you could see and learn for yourself how to create beautiful things in Photoshop. I took that approach in this book as well, but on a slightly smaller scale. This time I interviewed four inspiring artists who work with Photoshop on the iPad in addition to Photoshop on the desktop: Ted Chin, Russell Brown, Frankie Cihi and Magdiel Lopez. Between the interviews, I put together very efficient lessons in which you'll get to work with Photoshop on the iPad and accompanying apps. This will give you a full picture of Photoshop on the iPad and also teach you how to create beautiful images. Doing is the best way to learn!

Who's this book for?

This book is for anyone who wants to learn how to work with Photoshop on the iPad, whether you're a beginner or an advanced user of Photoshop on the desktop. I've found that people without Photoshop knowledge find their way around this app pretty quickly. But to get the most out of it they do need a little push. The advanced Photoshop user sometimes has to search for a favorite feature due to the new interface, but is usually positively surprised at what's possible. In the end, Photoshop on the iPad is great for anyone who wants to be able to work

© Russell Preston Brown

© Ted Chin

with Photoshop on the go, as well as designers and photographers who want to use the iPad to supplement their studio.

What will you learn?

This book isn't a manual. Manuals are boring and especially not inspiring at all. You'll only get to know a tool well by just using it. And above all, it should be fun when you learn how to work with it. Although this book isn't a manual, almost all of the functions and tools are covered in the various lessons. I've tried to make these lessons as fun and inspiring as possible. By the end of the book you'll have a complete overview of the capabilities of Photoshop on the iPad. As with Photoshop on the desktop, you can combine functions and tools endlessly. That sometimes feels intimidating, but makes it unlimited fun at the same time. Be sure to let me know what you thought of this book when you finish it. I wish you lots of fun and creativity!

Rob

robdewinter.com
dwmtrainingen.nl
youtube.com/robdewinter1
linkedin.com/in/robdewinter
instagram.com/robdewinter1
facebook.com/robdewinter1

Chapter 1

The start

Before you can start creating beautiful things in Photoshop on the iPad, you need to download a number of apps. These include the Adobe Creative Cloud app, as well as Lightroom Mobile and, of course, Photoshop on the iPad itself. In this chapter, you'll learn a bit about each one and how to put files on your iPad. Plus, I'll answer the most frequently asked questions about Photoshop on the iPad.

Which iPad apps?

This book is, of course, about Photoshop on the iPad. But to get the most out of this app, you may also find it useful to download a number of other apps from the Apple App Store. Together they turn your iPad into a complete creative workstation. The apps used in this book are discussed in the following sections. You'll also find more information about the various Creative Cloud subscriptions.

Photoshop on the iPad and subscriptions

You can download Photoshop on the iPad from the App Store (**Figure 1.01**), but to activate the app you'll need one of the Creative Cloud subscriptions. A subscription allows you to create an Adobe ID so you can log in to all your Adobe applications.

The range and price of these subscriptions can vary. Therefore, I recommend checking Adobe's website for current prices and bundles: **www.adobe.com**.

Currently, the cheapest option is the *Photography plan* for about $10 a month. With this subscription you get both desktop and iPad versions of Photoshop and Lightroom, lots of Creative Cloud storage space, access to Adobe Fonts and much more. This subscription offers by far the best value for money if you're a photographer and mainly use Photoshop and Lightroom.

The most complete, but also most expensive, subscription costs about $55 per month. For that price, you get all the Adobe desktop applications such as Illustrator, InDesign, Acrobat and Premiere Pro, as well as all the mobile applications and online services, such as Adobe Fonts.

You can also purchase a so-called *in-app subscription* right after downloading the app from the App Store. That subscription also costs about $10 a month and includes access to Photoshop on the iPad and the full, premium version of Adobe Fresco. I honestly think the in-app subscription is less attractive than the Photography plan in most cases.

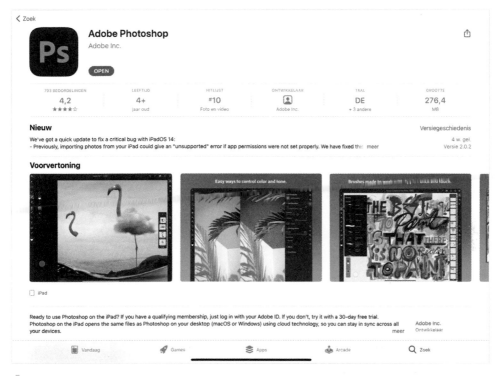

Figure 1.01 Photoshop on the iPad in the Apple App Store

Creative Cloud

The Creative Cloud app is one of those apps that makes you think at first: What do I need it for? Well, the app can actually do quite a lot. It lets you install premium fonts from Adobe Fonts on your iPad. And through the app, your iPad can access your Cloud Documents, Creative Cloud files and Libraries content. Cloud Documents are automatically saved when you work on a document in Photoshop on the iPad. You can easily open Cloud Documents from the Photoshop Home screen on the iPad, desktop and the web. This makes it very easy to quickly navigate back and forth between all your devices. Creative Cloud files are found in the iPad Files app and are therefore accessible in Photoshop and other apps. So install this app right away, because without it, you won't be able to open and save your files! You can download the Creative Cloud app from the App Store, and we'll talk about how to put files on your iPad near the end of this chapter.

Adobe Lightroom

There's also a mobile iPad version available for Adobe Lightroom (**Figure 1.02**). The app is largely free to use. If you already have a Creative Cloud subscription, such as the Photography plan, even more features are unlocked. This Lightroom app works perfectly with the Photoshop app. Even though Photoshop on the iPad can now edit raw photos, I regularly use Lightroom to edit photos before sending them to Photoshop or to post-edit a photo composition from Photoshop. You'll learn how to do that later in this book.

Figure 1.02 Lightroom on the iPad

Adobe Capture

This is one of my favorite apps. Capture recognizes fonts and creates color themes, brushes, patterns and shapes. I use Capture mostly on my iPhone, but there's also an iPad version. You won't need the app right away when you get started with this book. But, while you're downloading apps anyway, you might as well install it for free.

Adobe Fresco

Adobe Fresco (**Figure 1.03**) is a drawing and painting app that lets you draw with many different vector brushes, pixel brushes and special brushes, such as watercolors and oils. It's an incredibly intuitive app that works very well with Photoshop on the iPad. For example, you can draw directly in your Photoshop files in Fresco, because Fresco documents automatically appear in Photoshop and vice versa. There's a free and a paid Fresco version available. With the paid version, you get a few extra features.

Adobe Illustrator

Since 2020, Adobe Illustrator has also been available on the iPad (**Figure 1.04**). We won't use the app in this book. If you already have a Creative Cloud subscription, however, it's worth getting this intuitive version of Illustrator on the iPad as well, so you can quickly design or edit vector drawings. After installing, you can also export your work for use in Photoshop on the iPad. As you have probably noticed, combining all the apps makes a powerful package.

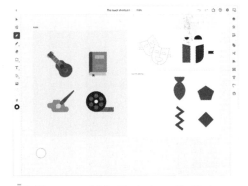

 Figure 1.03 Adobe Fresco   Figure 1.04 Adobe Illustrator on the iPad

Unsplash and Adobe Stock

Unsplash is the app from stock photo site **Unsplash.com**. Many Photoshop artists use this site to download royalty-free photos of fantastic quality to use in their work. If you regularly use photos in compositions or online materials, it's helpful to download Unsplash's app. There's also a fantastic free version of Adobe Stock available. You can find it at **stock.adobe.com/free**.

Which iPad and Apple Pencil?

Basically, Adobe Photoshop works on every iPad model Apple currently sells. For example, I recently tested the app on an iPad Mini 6, and it worked fine on that device too. Whether it really works comfortably is another question. In my opinion, the screen is rather small for all the various Photoshop functions.

iPad Pro and Apple Pencil 2

The configuration Adobe recommends for Photoshop is the iPad Pro with the 12.9-inch screen and the Apple Pencil 2 (**Figure 1.05**). I have that configuration myself, and it just works great. But, you do pay top dollar for this configuration, and in addition, I think the 12.9-inch iPad Pro is quite large. For photo editing and graphic design, the larger screen works wonderfully, but you're less likely to pick it up if you just want to go surf the web on your couch. I asked around a bit and heard that most professionals have the iPad Pro, with about half using the 11-inch version and the other half using the 12.9-inch version. I suggest trying out the different models in an Apple store first.

Figure 1.05 iPad Pro with Apple Pencil 2

The Apple Pencil 2 (**Figure 1.06**) currently works only on the following iPads:

» iPad Mini (6th generation)
» iPad Air (4th generation and later)
» iPad Pro 12.9-inch (3rd generation and later)
» iPad Pro 11-inch (1st generation and later)

Figure 1.06 Apple Pencil 2

With the Apple Pencil, you can draw, retouch, edit masks and much more with great precision and pressure sensitivity. It isn't recommended to control Photoshop on the iPad only with your fingers.

The big advantage of the Apple Pencil 2 is that you can charge it by magnetically sticking it to the top of compatible iPad models (**Figure 1.07**). That way, it also connects directly via Bluetooth. Also handy: because the Pencil 2 sticks magnetically to the iPad, you're less likely to lose it. Because it's flat on the charging side, it feels more like a real pencil, too.

Figure 1.07 The Apple Pencil 2 sticks magnetically and charges at the top of the iPad.

Other iPads and Apple Pencil 1

If you find the above iPad models too expensive or you prefer using a different type of iPad, then you can also choose one of these models and an Apple Pencil 1:

» iPad Mini (5th generation)
» iPad (6th, 7th, 8th, and 9th generation)

- » iPad (10th generation)*
- » iPad Air (3rd generation)
- » iPad Pro 12.9-inch (1st and 2nd generation)
- » iPad Pro 10.5-inch
- » iPad Pro 9.7-inch

Photoshop also runs on a few older iPad models, but the Apple Pencil no longer works on those. So I do not recommend those models.

The first stylus Apple released, the Apple Pencil 1 (**Figure 1.08**), draws just as well as the Apple Pencil 2, but it does have a few drawbacks. The Apple Pencil 1 is completely round, making it less comfortable to hold.

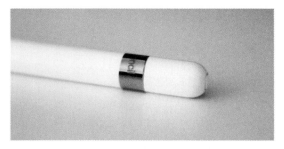

Figure 1.08 *You can recognize the Apple Pencil 1 by its metal rim.*

Furthermore, to charge the Pencil 1 you need to remove its mini-cap, which can get lost very quickly. Then you can use an adapter (also easily lost) to connect the Pencil to a charger or insert the back of the Pencil into the bottom of the iPad—a very fragile connection (**Figure 1.09**).

Figure 1.09 *Charging the Apple Pencil 1 is sometimes quite a hassle.*

The advantage is that the Pencil 1 is about $30 cheaper. If you already have an iPad that's compatible with the Pencil 1, then of course this is the most economical way to see if Photoshop on the iPad is for you.

Putting files on your iPad

Of course, if you're going to work with Photoshop on the iPad, it's important to be able to put photos or other images on your iPad. There are several ways to do that.

Via USB-C

All iPad models that are compatible with the Apple Pencil 2 (see page 7) have a USB-C connection. Many external hard drives today also have such a connection, allowing you to connect them directly to the iPad (**Figure 1.10**). The drive can then be accessed directly from the Adobe apps, or you can copy the files to the iPad using the Files app.

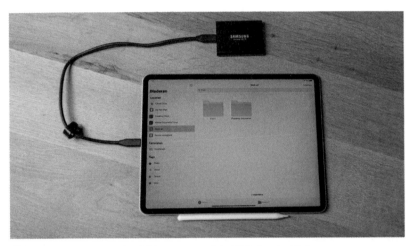

Figure 1.10 *External hard drive connected via USB-C to the iPad.*

Via a hub

You can also use a hub to which you can connect a memory card or regular USB drive (**Figure 1.11**). Newer and more expensive iPads require a USB-C connection, while older and cheaper models require a Lightning connection. This is especially useful if you want to copy your memory card from your camera directly to the iPad. Note: The more you want to use USB accessories, the more you should opt for an iPad with USB-C. Lightning is slower and has less power than USB-C. For example, to use a Lightning hub with storage and a card reader connected, the hub often needs to be powered by an external AC or battery power supply.

Figure 1.11 *A USB hub*

Via Cloud Documents and Creative Cloud Files

Saving and sharing files with other devices is by far the easiest via Cloud Documents. All files created in Photoshop on the iPad are automatically saved as a Photoshop Cloud Document with the extension *.psdc*. You don't have to do anything for this. As soon as you start Photoshop on your computer, the documents from your iPad immediately appear in the Photoshop Home screen. When you click a document, the file is downloaded, and you can continue working on your computer. And, when you save a Cloud Document in Photoshop on the desktop, it automatically appears in Photoshop on the iPad as well (**Figure 1.12**). You'll see examples of this process throughout this book.

After installing the Creative Cloud app (see page 3) you can copy the exercise files from this book to your Creative Cloud Files for easy access in Photoshop. Creative Cloud Files is online storage, similar to services such as Dropbox, OneDrive and iCloud Drive. How to copy the exercise files to your Creative Cloud Files can be found on the first pages of this book.

Figure 1.12 Photoshop on the iPad Home screen

Via your camera

These days, many camera brands have their own app that lets you transfer photos and videos to your phone or iPad via Wi-Fi. You can also pair most cameras with your iPad via USB or Bluetooth.

Frequently asked questions

I can imagine you still have a few questions about Photoshop on the iPad. People I talk to often do. Here are a few of the questions I hear most frequently.

Does Photoshop on the iPad also run on an Android tablet?
No, there's no Android app available at this time.

What iPad model runs Photoshop?
See page 6. Because some things change from time to time, I'd also recommend keeping an eye on the Adobe and Apple websites before buying an iPad.

Is Photoshop on the iPad also available in other languages?
At the time of writing, Photoshop on the iPad is available in English, Czech, Danish, Dutch, Finnish, French, German, Italian, Japanese, Korean, Norwegian, Polish, Portuguese, Russian, Simplified Chinese, Spanish, Swedish, Traditional Chinese and Turkish.

Is there much difference between Photoshop on the iPad and Photoshop on the desktop?
Yes and no. Both versions consist of the exact same code. But, because the iPad is a completely different device, the creators completely redesigned the app to be better suited for a smaller touchscreen. As a result, you'll probably miss some features. It was never intended to be a one-to-one copy of the Photoshop desktop version. Some options will probably never be added, but I don't think that's a big problem. For those advanced options you'll probably keep going to the desktop version anyway. You'll mostly use the iPad for specific things that a touchscreen is better at.

Who is Photoshop on the iPad for?
I think there'll be roughly two types of users who will enjoy reading this book: experienced users of the desktop version of Photoshop and people who've never worked with Photoshop before. For the experienced group, Photoshop on the iPad will be a great addition—not only for use on the go or in a studio, but also because

the iPad version works much more intuitively in some areas, like retouching, masking and painting. The seamless combination with apps like Fresco allows you to draw and paint very realistically in your Photoshop files. In this case, the iPad app can be a very nice addition to a standard (graphic) work environment and not only because of its mobile use.

For the second, less-experienced group of users, Photoshop on the iPad can be a very nice start. The desktop version can be quite intimidating and difficult for a new user, while the iPad version is incredibly intuitive. The experienced Photoshop user sometimes has to take a little time to find their way around the simplified iPad interface, while a new user usually knows their way around right away. Knowing the iPad app well over time can be a nice stepping stone to start using the desktop version of Photoshop.

How does Photoshop on the desktop work with Photoshop on the iPad?
When you create a document on the iPad, it automatically syncs with the cloud every few minutes. The moment you open Photoshop on the desktop, the iPad document is immediately available in the Home screen, allowing you to continue working in your document immediately. Vice versa, this works the same way if the document was saved from Photoshop on the desktop as a Photoshop Cloud Document.

Furthermore, you can also save your desktop documents in a Creative Cloud folder or in another cloud environment and open them again on the iPad.

Can I also use keyboard shortcuts?
Yes, if you connect a keyboard to the iPad, you can also use some common keyboard shortcuts (such as copy and paste). If you hold down the Command key when Photoshop is open, all available keyboard shortcuts are displayed. There's also a touch shortcut available. That's a round button in the Photoshop screen. You can use this button to simulate the Shift and Alt keys. You'll read more about that later in this book.

If Photoshop on the iPad is so intuitive, why do I need to read this book?

Haha, that's a good question! Photoshop on the iPad is indeed a very intuitive program. In fact, I think you'll be able to get along with it pretty quickly, even without this book.

Still, if you want to achieve the same results as in Photoshop on the desktop, you'll sometimes have to think in a different way. This is mainly because the interface looks different, but also because some options you know from the desktop version are not (yet) available on the iPad. This encourages creative thinking, often allowing you to achieve your end result in a simpler way. And sometimes it allows you to achieve an even more beautiful end result. In any case, with this book I want to offer you inspiration and an amazing overview of all the possibilities in Photoshop on the iPad.

Does this book contain sponsored elements?

No. I wrote this book because I've been an avid Photoshop user and teacher for years and now see really great possibilities with Photoshop on the iPad. I often work with Adobe and with the Adobe Photoshop team, but I only do that because I think it's super fun to do and because I think it's an amazing product, made by incredibly talented people. Apps, iPads, Apple Pencils and other services covered in this book are shown because I'm enthusiastic about them myself and use them to my complete satisfaction.

Have fun following the exercises and reading the inspiring interviews. Time to get started!

Chapter 2

Photoshop basics

PHOTOSHOP ON THE IPAD INTERFACE AND BASICS

A tidy new interface designed specifically for the iPad: As an advanced Photoshop user, it takes some getting used to. And as a new user, sometimes you don't know your way around right away either. That's why we'll first take a look at the Photoshop on the iPad interface. Then we'll cover the most important Photoshop basics and some very handy touch shortcuts.

Getting oriented

If you've worked with Photoshop on the desktop before, the interface of the iPad version suddenly looks a lot simpler and more compact. Despite that compact interface, you can still find many familiar options. In the following sections, we'll go through all the options so you know exactly where to find them.

By the way, from now on I'll just call Photoshop on the iPad *Photoshop* in most cases. When I refer to the desktop version, I'll call it *Photoshop on the desktop*.

The Home screen

Figure 2.01 The Photoshop Home screen

After opening Photoshop, you'll be taken directly to the Home screen (**Figure 2.01**). Here you'll find all your recently opened files.

On the left side of this Home screen you'll find a column of buttons. Here's where they'll take you when you tap:

HOME: The Home screen is the first screen you see when you open Photoshop. From this screen you can open all your recent Cloud Documents, view tutorials, open a file stored on your iPad or online, or create a new file.

LEARN: In this very useful section you'll find tutorials and lessons. Some of these tutorials give you an in-app tour around Photoshop. Others will just show you a video.

DISCOVER: This fun section is a great source of inspiration. Watch recordings of livestreams and see projects that other artists have created in Photoshop. The Discover section is linked to **Behance.net**, Adobe's portfolio site.

YOUR FILES: Here you'll find all the Cloud Documents you created in Photoshop or in Adobe Fresco. If the Home screen is empty after a fresh new installation of Photoshop, you can always go to this section.

SHARED WITH YOU: If someone has shared a Cloud Document with you, it'll show up in this section.

DELETED: Here you'll find a list of all Cloud Documents that you have deleted. You can also choose to restore the documents or permanently delete them.

CREATE NEW: In this section you can create a new document and set options for it. You'll find several document presets here.

IMPORT AND OPEN: Here you can choose to open documents from the Photos app, Files app or iPad camera:
»   If your file is in the Photos app, tap *Photos*. Pictures you took with the iPad camera, and photos synced via iCloud, are stored here.
»   If your file is in the Files app, tap *Files*. This is also how you open files from an external hard drive or card reader, or documents in

the synced Creative Cloud folder.

» If you want to use the iPad camera to create a new Photoshop document, tap *Camera*.

An imported file automatically converts to a Photoshop Cloud Document that can be opened seamlessly from all your devices. If you want to open a Photoshop Cloud Document created on your computer, tap it in the *Recent* list in the Home screen.

The Edit workspace

Before we cover the Edit workspace, let's open a file first. If you transferred the exercise files to your iPad using the instructions on page iii, they will be in the Files app, so we'll open them from there.

1. To open a Photoshop file, tap the *Import and Open* button on the Home screen; then tap *Files* (**Figure 2.02**) to open the file browser.

Figure 2.02 Open a file.

2. Navigate to the exercise files folder, go to *Chapter 2* and select the file *ps-ipad-interface.psd* (**Figure 2.03**).

Figure 2.03 Open the file via Import and Open > Files.

Once the file is loaded, the Edit workspace and the document appear automatically (**Figure 2.04**).

Header bar

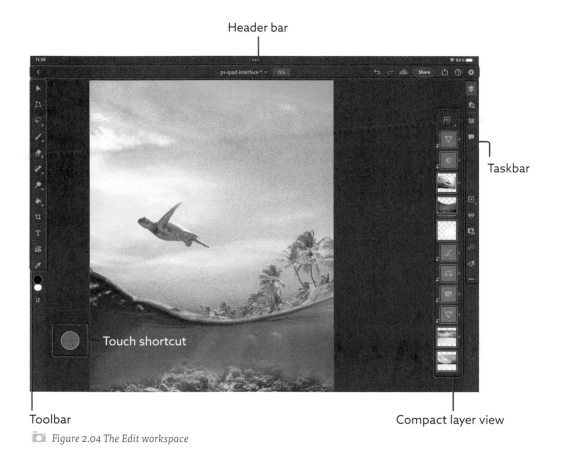

Taskbar

Touch shortcut

Toolbar

Compact layer view

Figure 2.04 The Edit workspace

Let's take a look at each section of the Edit workspace more closely.

HEADER BAR: This bar is found at the top of your screen. On the left is the button to return to the Home screen ⬅, and on the far right are some general buttons to undo actions ↩ ↪, share and export your files ⬆, get help ⓘ and view the current document settings ⚙. In the center you'll find the document name `ps-ipad-interface` and zoom percentage `71%`. A few tips: Double-tap the zoom percentage to zoom your canvas to fit the screen. Tapping again takes you back to the previous zoom percentage. By tapping the document name, you can change the file name or save the file.

TOOLBAR: This is the bar where you'll find all the tools (**Figure 2.05**); this bar has many similarities to the toolbar in Photoshop on the desktop. Tapping a tool activates it. Some tools (such as the Lasso tool) have a small triangle at their bottom right, indicating more tools are available. You can find them by double-tapping the tool or by tapping and holding the tool down a little longer. The book's exercises will cover most of these tools.

TOUCH SHORTCUT: The touch shortcut allows you to mimic the most common modifier keys. For example, in Photoshop on the desktop, you often use the Shift or Alt key (Option on macOS) to duplicate objects or to switch between erase and draw when working with a brush. Those keys aren't present on the iPad, so Adobe added the touch shortcut. You press it with one finger while working with another finger or the Apple Pencil on the canvas. The touch shortcut has two behaviors:

Tap and hold the center: This is the primary touch shortcut (**Figure 2.06**). You use it to modify the most common tasks, like moving on the X/Y axis and snapping rotation to 15 degrees.

Tap and slide from the center to the outer ring: This is the secondary touch shortcut (**Figure 2.06**). You usually use it to modify less common—but no less convenient—tasks, like duplicating while moving and scaling from the center.

Figure 2.05
The toolbar

 Figure 2.06 Primary touch shortcut (left) and secondary touch shortcut (right)

It usually does exactly what you expect, but to get the most out of the touch shortcut you'll find all the possible combinations later in this chapter. By the way, if you have a keyboard connected to the iPad, you can hold down the Command key when Photoshop is open. All available keyboard shortcuts will then be displayed.

TASKBAR: The taskbar (**Figure 2.07**) can be found on the right side of the window. The upper part of the bar contains the buttons you use to access the Compact or Detailed layer view, the layer properties and the comments section. The lower part contains a range of layer actions, like creating a new layer or a new adjustment layer, adding a layer mask, applying effects and performing more layer actions that pop up when you tap the three dots at the very bottom.

Compact layer view

Detail layer view

Layer Properties

Comments

Add layer

Layer visibility

Add layer mask

Add clipping mask

Filters and adjustments

More layer actions

Figure 2.07 Taskbar overview

LAYER VIEWS: Photoshop on the iPad has two layer views: *Compact layer view* (**Figure 2.08**) and *Detail layer view* (**Figure 2.09**). Both layer views are linked to the top two buttons in the taskbar. I usually work with the detailed version because I find I have a better overview of all the layers there. If you work on a small iPad screen, it might be more practical to work with Compact layer view.

Figure 2.08 Compact layer view   Figure 2.09 Detail layer view

LAYER PROPERTIES: This is the panel in which you see all available layer properties for the selected layer or layer group. The panel is dynamic: If you tap a regular pixel layer, you'll see the options for pixel layers (**Figure 2.10**). If you tap an adjustment layer, you'll see the options for that adjustment layer (**Figure 2.11**). This works much like the Properties panel you may have used in many Adobe Creative Cloud desktop applications. By the way, if this is your first time opening Photoshop, this may suddenly look very complicated. Don't worry, all the elements will be covered step by step later.

Figure 2.10 Pixel layer properties

Figure 2.11 Adjustment layer properties

Figure 2.12
Tool options

TOOL OPTIONS: If additional settings are available for the selected tool, they'll appear in the Tool Options panel (**Figure 2.12**). For example, if you selected the Brush tool, this panel appears. You can then adjust the brush size or the brush hardness and a number of other settings. Or with the Lasso tool selected, you'll see various selection options. Tip: You can move the Tool Options panel by dragging the top edge of the panel.

ACTIVE SELECTION PROPERTIES This bar with all the selection properties appears automatically when you create a selection. Think of a selection with the Lasso tool (**Figure 2.13**). Once you've made a selection, you'll find all available actions in this bar, such as for deselecting, inverting or masking the selection. One of these options is my favorite feature, Refine Edge, which allows you to select hair and other "thin" objects. (In Photoshop on the desktop, you'll find this feature under Select and Mask.) When you tap the More button, you'll even find more options.

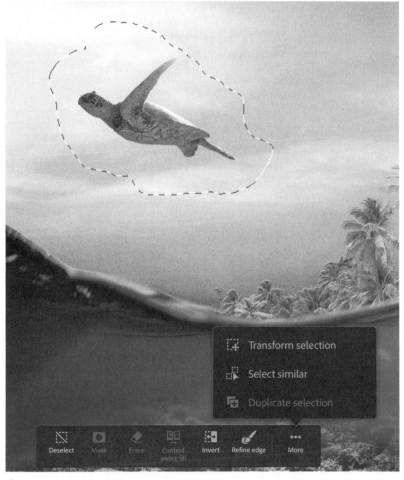

Figure 2.13 Active Selection Properties

How do layers work?

You can use Photoshop without adding layers, but layers provide so much of the power of Photoshop that they're well worth learning. Somehow, many people already panic a little when I start talking about layers, but fortunately they're really not that difficult.

Stacked objects

Photoshop offers more than one kind of layer. For example, you have text layers, pixel layers and adjustment layers. The basic principle of all these types of layers remains the same: Each layer has its own place in the *layer stack*. For example, if you put a very large photo on top of all the layers, you're likely not to see the other layers. This is because the top layer covers all the layers below it. If you were to move that very large top photo to the bottom of the stack, you would see the other layers.

Figure 2.14 shows well how layer order works. In the Compact layer view on the right, you can see that Layer 4, which contains the orange square, is on top of the layer stack. The same orange square is also "on top" in your image. Whenever you aren't sure about the structure of your Photoshop document, always look at the layers in your Layers panel first.

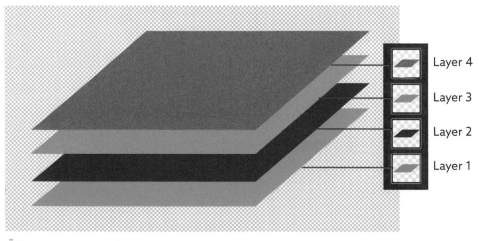

Figure 2.14 Layer order

In **Figure 2.15**, you can see some stacked layers in the Photoshop Layers panel. By stacking the layers in this way, the sea (the Sea Group layers) and the trees (the Trees layer) are in front of the sky (the Sky layer). Later you'll learn more about the different layer types, but you can already see how the layers are arranged.

Figure 2.15 A layer example in Photoshop on the iPad

Layer order

You can very easily change the order of layers by dragging one or more layers up or down in the Layers panel (**Figure 2.16**). Just tap and hold the layer, drag it up or down, and release where you want it. So if you want to quickly move a layer to the back, just drag it down. Want something in the foreground? Drag the layer up.

Figure 2.16 Tap and hold a layer to drag it up or down.

What are adjustment layers?

In the coming chapters you'll encounter adjustment layers a lot. For now, it's important that you understand the basics a little; then the rest will come later.

An *adjustment layer* applies edits, such as brightness and contrast, to underlying layers. When you create an adjustment layer, it's added on top of the selected layer (**Figure 2.17**). Then you can set the adjustments in the Layer Properties panel. This panel usually opens automatically when you add an adjustment layer, but you'll

Figure 2.17 The Layers and Layer Properties panels

notice that you usually have it open by default anyway because you tapped the corresponding button ⚏ in the toolbar earlier. Later you'll see how to create your own adjustment layer.

In the Layers panel in **Figure 2.17**, you can see a number of adjustment layers, such as Color Balance 1 and Vibrance 3. These adjust color balance and a tint change, respectively, in the layers below. Notice that Color Balance 1 is selected in the Layers panel. As a result, you see the settings for the Color Balance 1 layer in the Layer Properties panel, too.

By adjusting the settings in the Layer Properties panel, you can change how an adjustment layer changes the layers below it. In this case, however, only the Trees layer (the second layer from below) changes. This is because the three layers above it (Color Balance 1, Photo Filter 1 and Vibrance 3) are *clipped adjustment layers*. You can recognize them by the small arrows to the left of the layer icon (**Figure 2.18**). A clipped adjustment layer is applied only to the layer directly below it.

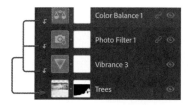

Figure 2.18 Clipped adjustment layers

You can add as many adjustment layers as you like. In **Figure 2.17** you can see several more adjustment layers in the Layers panel. A newly created adjustment layer automatically stacks on top of the selected layer. Best of all, you can always adjust the effects afterwards in the Layer Properties panel or turn them off by tapping the Layer Visibility (eye) icon to the right of the layer name in the Layers panel.

You can find more about adjustment layers and their settings in later exercises in this book.

What are layer masks?

Layer masks are one of the most useful and versatile things in Photoshop. Once you know how layer masks work, you'll use them in every Photoshop project. Especially in the iPad version of Photoshop, they are extremely useful. In fact, you can't work without them. Masks will come back a lot in this book, so that's why in this chapter I'll just briefly show you what a layer mask is.

Black and white

With a *layer mask*, you control which areas in a layer are transparent and which aren't. Imagine that little black-and-white rectangle in **Figure 2.19** is actually on top of the layer with the sea turtle. All black areas would be transparent, and all white parts would be shown, so you could see only the sea turtle in the image. That's why the rhyme *"Black conceals, white reveals"* is how many Photoshop users remember how layer masks work. We want the background to disappear and the turtle to remain, so the turtle is white while the rest of the layer is black in the mask.

Figure 2.19 A layer mask shown in Detail layer view

Compare what the image looks like before adding a layer mask (**Figure 2.20**) and after (**Figure 2.21**). As you can see, the layer mask removes the background of the turtle image so it fits seamlessly in the scene.

You can create a layer mask in several ways. One such way is to click the Layer Mask button ▣ in the taskbar.

Once you tap the Layer Mask thumbnail to the right of the layer thumbnail in the Detail layer view, the mask is active, and you can start working in it. If you paint with a black brush, for example, the areas you paint over become transparent (because black conceals).

Figure 2.20 Without a layer mask

Figure 2.21 With a layer mask

If you paint with a white brush, you "paint back" parts of the layer (because white reveals). We'll do this many more times in the exercises, so if you don't quite understand the mask principle yet, it'll be clear later.

One more thing: If you're working in the Compact layer view, you can activate the layer mask by swiping the layer thumbnail to the left (**Figure 2.22**).

These were just the basic options for layer masks. The possibilities are endless. I hope to get you excited about all the possibilities in this book.

Figure 2.22 Activate a layer mask in Compact layer view.

Select and move layers

You can select and move layers with the Move tool. Nowadays, the Auto-Select Layer on Canvas option is activated by default. This option automatically selects the layer on which you tap on the canvas.

1. Select the *Move tool* ▶.
2. Open the Move Tool Settings panel by tapping the three dots in the Tool Options panel. You'll see that *Auto-Select Layer on Canvas* is enabled by default (**Figure 2.23**).
3. Tap the turtle on the canvas. Transform handles appear. You can now move, scale or rotate the turtle (**Figure 2.24**).

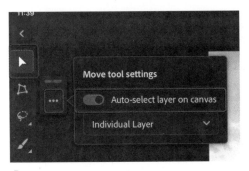

Figure 2.23 Move tool settings

Figure 2.24 The turtle layer is selected.

4. Tap outside (or on) the turtle again, and notice that the transform handles disappear but the layer is still selected in the Layers panel. In this mode, you can easily move the layer without accidentally transforming it with the handles.
5. If you now tap another layer on the canvas, that layer will be selected. Try this by tapping the sea layer.
6. Tap outside or on the sea layer: The transformation handles disappear, but the sea layer is still selected in the Layers panel. If you tap another layer, that layer is selected, and so on.

So it's important to understand that, with Auto-Select Layer on Canvas activated, the first tap selects a layer, the second tap hides the transform handles but keeps the layer selected, and the third tap on another layer selects that layer.

If you don't like this behavior and don't want to auto-select layers, you can follow these steps:

1. In the Move Tool Settings panel (**Figure 2.23**) tap *Auto-Select Layer on Canvas* to disable layer auto-select.
2. Select the layer you want to move or edit in the Layers panel.
3. Move the layer on the canvas.

Remember, every time you want to select, move or edit a layer, you have to select it in the Layers panel first.

I actually like the auto-select behavior, so I leave Auto-Select Layer on Canvas enabled.

Grouped layers

Grouped layers look slightly different on the iPad than on the desktop. You recognize them by a little arrow to the left of the layer thumbnail (**Figure 2.25**). Tapping that arrow opens the layer group, allowing you to see and edit its contents.

Figure 2.25 The opened Sea Group in the Layers panel. The Sea layer is selected.

Many other things are possible with layers. We'll cover those possibilities in the various lessons in this book. At least you now have an impression of the most common options.

Photoshop gestures

Photoshop on the iPad is a touch application. Therefore, you can use gestures to perform quick actions, like undo or zooming in and out. This enables you to work much faster with Photoshop. You'll find a list of all gestures under the Help button ⊙ in the Edit workspace, but here's a quick guide to the gestures you'll use most.

Undo
Two-finger tap

Redo
Three-finger tap

Reveal more options
Double-tap or long-press icons that have triangles on the bottom right

Zoom, rotate and pan canvas
Pinch to zoom
Twist to rotate
Two-finger drag to pan

Fit to view
Quick pinch

View at 100%
Double-tap

Touch shortcut

As you may remember, the touch shortcut has a primary behavior (controlled by the inner ring) and a secondary behavior (controlled by the outer ring). When you press the primary or secondary touch shortcut and it applies to the current tool or mode, a blue tool tip in the upper-right corner of the screen tells you what the shortcut does. Here's another tip: You can also slide the touch shortcut to another place on your screen. This is useful, for example, if you are left-handed. Just hold the touch shortcut and then drag it away. What else can the touch shortcut do? A lot, depending on the tool you combine it with. You'll find a list of all touch shortcuts under the Help button ⊙ in the Edit workspace, but here's a quick guide to common ones.

Tool	Primary touch shortcut	Secondary touch shortcut
▶ **Move**	Move on the X/Y axis	Duplicate
⟦⟧ **Transform: Scale**	Scale unproportionally	Scale from center
↺ **Transform: Rotate**	Snap to 15 degrees	*None*
⟆ **Lasso**	Add to selection	*None*
⟆ **Quick Selection and Object Selection**	Subtract from selection	*None*
⬚ **Marquee Rectangle**	Select with square	Select from the center with square
◌ **Marquee Ellipse**	Select with circle	Select from the center with circle
✎ **Brush**	Eraser	Eyedropper
⚲ **Clone Stamp**	Set source	*None*
⌗ **Crop**	Crop proportionally	Crop proportionally from the center
Layers	Tap a layer or layer group to select multiple layers	

Chapter 3

Ted Chin

PHOTOSHOPPING FOR PHOTOSHOP

If you're a Photoshop user, you know Ted Chin from the flamingo artwork used in the Photoshop 2021 splash screen. Ted is originally from Taiwan. Through a student exchange program, after several years of study in New York, he ended up at the Art Institute in San Francisco. After that study, he continued to live in San Francisco and now creates work for companies such as Adobe and Facebook. He enjoys California's forests, mountains and water immensely, and he plans to live in the United States for years to come.

Name:	Ted Chin
Residence:	San Francisco, USA
Finds inspiration:	Through close observation
Favorite tool:	Select Subject
Most used tools:	Select Subject, Refine Edge, masks, selections and brushes
Other favorites:	Lightroom Mobile and Pixelsquid
Best advice:	Make the things you really like and learn all about light, shadow, perspective and color

How do you use Photoshop on the iPad?

For me, it always starts with the idea. Sometimes I get inspired by an image I've seen somewhere. I think of all kinds of ideas in my head until I come up with a new concept. I then develop that concept by searching stock photo sites for images that I can use for that idea. Once I find those images, I create a new Photoshop document with a 4:5 ratio. That ratio works best on social media platforms, but also works well if you have a photo or composition printed. I then import all the collected images into the new document, making selections and masks and moving objects back and forth until I have created the composition I had in mind.

I mainly work with Photoshop on the iPad when I'm on the road or when I can't use my laptop. I traveled a lot. On those trips I only had my iPad with me and did all my work on it in the car on the way. I also use Photoshop on the iPad in my studio to complement Photoshop on the desktop. I sketch ideas on it or work out basic ideas. Photoshop on the iPad works very intuitively, making it easier to experiment with ideas if I can't figure it out on the desktop.

© Ted Chin

© Ted Chin

Photoshop on the iPad does not yet include all the features from the desktop version. Do you occasionally feel limited when working with Photoshop on the iPad?

Very occasionally, yes. On the other hand, I've also seen that people who only have a very small amount of knowledge of Photoshop on the desktop find the iPad version a relief. They can create beautiful things with it pretty quickly. Not all the desktop features are present on the iPad, but maybe that's precisely why it's so incredibly intuitive and makes it easier to focus on the parts that really matter. And, the most missed desktop features will soon be added on the iPad anyway.

Do you sometimes combine other apps with Photoshop?
Yes, I use the Lightroom for iPad app mainly for initial, global editing of my raw or JPG files. For example, I darken or lighten the photos and increase or decrease the contrast so that they then fit better into my photo composition. Then I send the photo from Lightroom to Photoshop and create the composite image there.

I also use the *Pixelsquid* app. This app allows you to place ready-made 3D objects created by other designers into your composition. The handy thing about Pixelsquid is that you can rotate 3D objects at all sorts of angles until the model fits exactly into the composition. You can use either the Pixelsquid iPad app or the Photoshop desktop plug-in.

What iPad are you currently working on?
The largest (12.9-inch) iPad Pro with an Apple Pencil 2. It works great. I love the big screen and wouldn't want a smaller one.

© Ted Chin

© Ted Chin

Are there other artists who inspire you?

Yes for sure, there are almost too many artists to mention. My all-time favorites are Hayao Miyazaki's anime films. Some of my favorite surrealist artists are René Magritte, Salvador Dalí, Man Ray and photographers such as Erik Almas, Erik Johansson and Benjamin Von Wong. I also like painters like Vladimir Kush, Rhads and Aquasixio. Lately, I've also been watching Benny Productions' speed editing tutorials on YouTube a lot.

Where do you get the images for your photo compositions?

Especially from stock photo sites like Unsplash and Adobe Stock. I also enjoy taking my own photos. These are mainly photos of models that I integrate into my compositions. I also create my own Photoshop brushes. With these brushes I can draw fog, water, splashes or hair.

If I don't make the brushes myself, I use the standard Photoshop brushes or download them from various websites. There are lots of free brushes out there. I also created a catalog of standard image assets. In this catalog, for example, I have an image with white snowflakes on a black background. When I need snow in a composition, I place that photo on top of my Photoshop document, set the blend mode to Screen so you don't see the black colors anymore, but you can still see the snowflakes. Very handy!

What are your favorite tools in Photoshop on the iPad?

I think *Select Subject* and *Refine Edge* are very useful tools. Because these tools use artificial intelligence, they save me a lot of time. That these two tools allow me to select objects and hair so easily and quickly on an iPad is almost magical.

Do you have any tips for new users?

I certainly have. My first tip is to primarily do the things you really enjoy. I love creating beautiful, imaginative photo compositions, so that's what I focus on the most. Never forget that you don't create your work for social media, but because you enjoy designing or photographing yourself. I'm always reminded of a photographer who told me that he's very satisfied if he makes 10 great photos in one year—even though he photographs all year round. You can only do something like that if you really enjoy your work. The second tip is that, especially in Photoshop on the iPad, you should use layer masks a lot. Without masks, you're nowhere. And, learn how light, shadow, perspective and color work. Those are the basics where the magic begins. Everyone is familiar with light, shadow, perspective and color, yet it takes quite a bit of time and effort to be able to apply it properly when creating photo compositions.

© Ted Chin

© Ted Chin

Chapter 4

Photo composition

COMPOSING IMAGES ON THE IPAD

In this first lesson, we begin by creating a magical photo composition inspired by the work of Ted Chin. It's a fairly long exercise, where lots of features of Photoshop on the iPad pass by. After following this lesson, you will have created a beautiful composition, and you'll also see that you can create fantastic images with Photoshop on the iPad with relatively few tools!

The photo composition

In this first "real" tutorial chapter, you'll learn how to create the composition you see on the next page. When I teach Photoshop courses, I always find that the best way to learn software is by doing, not by reading through a manual. After all, in a manual you won't find many practical exercises.

Inspired by the work of Ted Chin (**Figure 4.01**), in this exercise we'll combine a large number of tools and techniques in a very efficient way, eventually giving you the beautiful end result shown in **Figure 4.02**. By combining as many tools and different kinds of images as possible, you will immediately have a good overview of the possibilities in Photoshop on the iPad.

Good luck and most of all have fun!

Figure 4.01 Ted Chin's original artwork

Figure 4.02 *The end result*

A new Photoshop document

Let's get started. Just as Ted Chin usually does, we'll first create a new document with a 4:5 ratio, which in this case will be 3000 by 3750 pixels. In this document we'll place several images, remove the background and much more.

1. Open Photoshop and tap *Create New* at the bottom left of the Home screen.
2. Choose the *Print* tab and a preset such as the *1000 pixel grid*. After that, change the document size to *3000 by 3750 pixels* (**Figure 4.03**).

To determine the 4:5 ratio, I first determined the width: 3000 pixels. You can print this width at 10 inches, as well as post it on social media with good quality. Then I divided 3000 by 4, and multiplied it by 5 to determine the height.

3. Tap *Create* in the lower-right corner. A new document will be created.

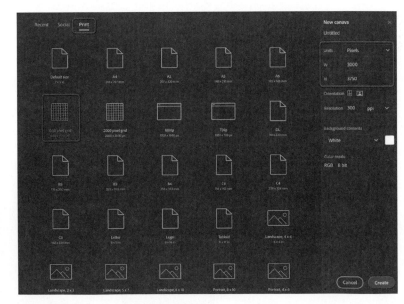

Figure 4.03 Create a new document at dimensions you specify.

Place images

Because the photo composition consists of several photos, in this step we'll begin by placing a background image. If you haven't already, you'll need to download the exercise files for this chapter, following the instructions at the beginning of this book.

1. Tap the *Place Photo* button. If your files are stored in the Creative Cloud folder or on your iPad, choose *Files*. Find the folder for this chapter and select the image *sky* (**Figure 4.04**).

Figure 4.04 *Place an image.*

2. After the file downloads, Photoshop takes you to the *Transform* window where you can transform the image by dragging the handles in the corners. The most efficient way to fill the document height is to, in the same single action, drag a side or corner handle while holding down the secondary touch shortcut to scale proportionally from the center (**Figure 4.05**).

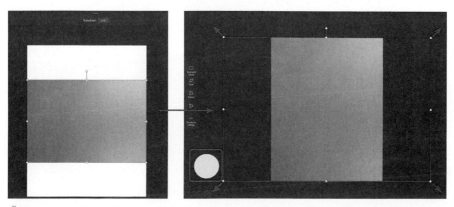

Figure 4.05 *Resize the image. Hold the secondary touch shortcut to scale from the center.*

3. Tap *Done* when you're finished. Now, you're back in the Edit workspace and the imported image becomes a new layer.

4. Place the next image in exactly the same way. Tap the *Place Photo* tool again, choose *Files* and then choose *stars* (**Figure 4.06**).

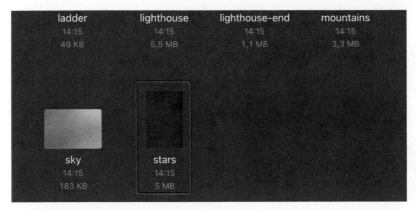

Figure 4.06 Place the stars image.

5. This time enlarge the image until it is slightly larger than the canvas and tap *Done* (**Figure 4.07**).

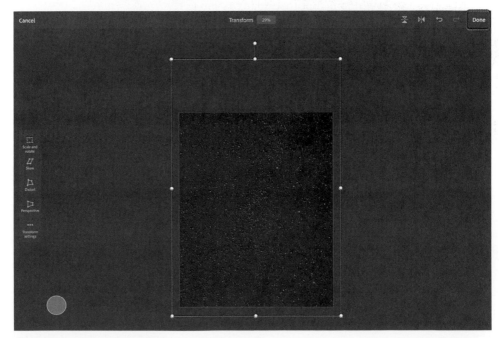

Figure 4.07 Transform the stars image.

6. Now open the *Detail layer view* and the *Layer Properties* panel by tapping the two corresponding buttons in the taskbar on the right side of the screen. These panels will give us some more options later (**Figure 4.08**).

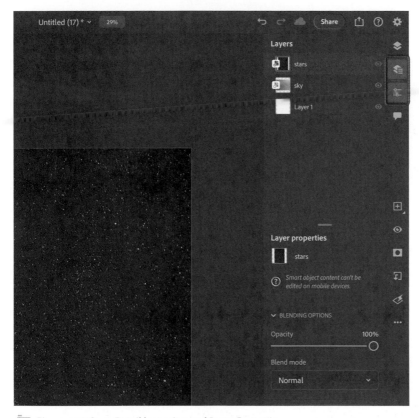

Figure 4.08 Open Detail layer view and Layer Properties.

As you may have seen in **Figure 4.02**, the starry sky blends much better into the background in the final result than it does right now. That's why we're going to use transparency and a blend mode. A blend mode is a way in which the top layer combines with the underlying layer, making that underlying layer visible again.

7. Make sure the top stars layer is still selected in the Layers panel. If it isn't, select the stars layer now. In the *Layer Properties* panel, we can now choose from a number of blend modes under *Blend mode* (**Figure 4.08**).

8. Open the *Blend mode* menu by tapping *Normal*. Eventually we'll choose the *Screen* option (**Figure 4.09**), but feel free to try out some other modes first to see exactly what they do.

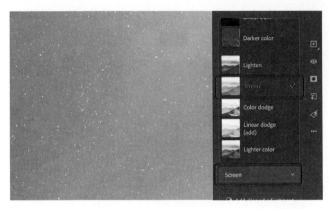

Figure 4.09 Choose Screen blend mode.

By choosing *Screen*, all the blacks disappear from the top star image, and only the stars and other light objects shine through on the underlying layer. In this case, that underlying layer is the sky we placed first. The darker the top layer gets, the more transparent it becomes.

When applying blend modes, I usually run through all the options to see which mode gives the best results. It's often difficult to estimate exactly what a blend mode will do, because the effect depends on how dark or light, or how colorful or less colorful the top or bottom image is. You'll get opportunities to work with other blend modes coming up.

9. Finally, we need to make the stars a little more transparent because they're still too visible. To do this, slide the *Opacity* slider in the *Layer Properties* panel towards 20% (**Figure 4.10**).

Figure 4.10 Change Opacity to 20%.

Selections and masks

Now that the background is in the right place, it's time to place the mountain at the bottom of our composition. We'll remove the mountain's background by making a selection that we'll convert into a mask.

1. By now you know how to place an image: Tap the *Place Photo* button again, choose *Files* and select the file *mountains* (**Figure 4.11**).

Figure 4.11 Place mountains.jpg.

2. Make the image slightly larger and position it at the bottom of the image (**Figure 4.12**). When you're finished tap *Done*.

Figure 4.12 Scale and reposition the mountains.

You can remove a background in several ways, like using the automatic *Remove Background* function. But, in the next step we'll use the *Quick Selection tool* (**Figure 4.13**), because it gives you a little more control when selecting objects. Therefore, it's useful to master this tool rather than always rely on the automatic tools. We'll first create a selection and then a layer mask. With the Quick Selection tool, you simply draw over the object you want to select. Photoshop will then look for the edges of that object (in this case, the mountain). It's important to make sure there is sufficient contrast between the background and the object. If the selection edge accidentally jumps over the object, pressing the *touch shortcut* will allow you to "push back" (Subtract) the edges by drawing over the over-selected areas. If you're used to the desktop version of Photoshop, this concept is similar to holding down the Alt key (or Option on macOS).

Figure 4.13
Quick Selection tool

3. Activate the *Quick Selection tool* by tapping and holding the Lasso tool—or one of the other active selection tools—for a moment, or tapping it twice (**Figure 4.14**). The selection tools collapse. Now select the third tool 🖊, the *Quick Selection tool*.

4. Before you start selecting, make the selection brush a little larger. If the brush is larger, Photoshop will also select faster. Here's a handy trick you can use to make the brush larger: Use your Apple Pencil or finger to go to the brush size in the *Tools Options* panel (**Figure 4.15**). Then tap, hold and immediately drag upwards to make the brush size larger or downwards to make it smaller. I made my brush about *130 pixels* in size.

Figure 4.14 Quick Selection tool

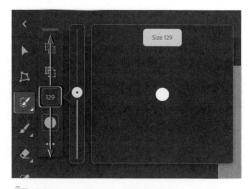

Figure 4.15 Change the brush size.

5. The brush is now large enough. Draw over the mountain to select it. Never draw over the outer edge of the mountain, because that'll select the sky. Sometimes you may have to draw closer to the mountain's edge to include all the edges (**Figure 4.16**). You don't have to get the selection right in just one stroke. As long as the selection is still active, you can draw as many times as you need to add to or subtract from the selection. Also, feel free to zoom in to check the selection edge more closely.

📷 *Figure 4.16 Tap, hold and drag the Quick Selection tool.*

TIP: Made a mistake? Tap with two fingers to undo the action. Tapping with three fingers will redo the action again. See page 32 for all Photoshop gestures.

6. As you can see in **Figure 4.17**, my selection still has a small edge of sky selected along with it. Remove any leftover bits like this by pressing the center of the *touch shortcut* and then drawing over that edge. The touch shortcut activates the *Subtract from Selection* function, allowing you to deselect parts of your selection (**Figure 4.17**).

📷 *Figure 4.17 Subtract by holding the primary touch shortcut.*

7. If you are completely happy with your selection, create a layer mask. A mask hides everything outside your selection and shows everything inside it. To create a mask, tap the *Mask* button in the *Active Selection Properties* bar at the bottom of your screen (**Figure 4.18**).

TIP: If you're not satisfied with your original selection, you can also tap the *Deselect* button in this bar to deselect. You can then immediately start making a new selection.

Figure 4.18 Create a layer mask.

8. The mountain's background is now transparent. In the Layers panel, notice that a mask has been added to the mountains layer (**Figure 4.19**). All black parts are hidden, and all white parts are visible—*black conceals, white reveals*!

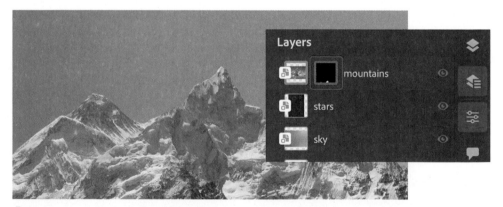

Figure 4.19 Layer mask in the Layers panel

Because the mask is perfect now, we won't do anything else with it at this point. In the next step, we'll adjust the way the mountain blends into the background.

9. There are several ways to make the color of the mountain match the background a little better. In this case, we'll use a blend mode again. Make sure the *Layer Properties* panel is open, then tap *Normal* under *Blend Mode* to open the list of blend modes and choose *Luminosity* (**Figure 4.20**). This is the last blend mode in the list.

Luminosity causes the top layer (the mountains) to adopt the colors (hue) and saturation of the colors from the layer below it (the sky), while maintaining the original exposure of the mountain.

10. Finally, lower the *Opacity* to about 70% (**Figure 4.20**). The extra transparency makes the mountain blend into the background even better.

📷 *Figure 4.20 Add a Luminosity blend mode.*

Learn more about blend modes

Want to read more about blend modes? Then take a look at the Adobe Help website:

helpx.adobe.com/photoshop/using/blending-modes.html

You can also scan the QR code to go to this website.

Select Subject and Refine Edge

Now that our background is all set, we can place the photo of the cloud and remove its background. To accomplish this, we're going to explore a selection feature named Select Subject.

1. First, go to *Place Photo* in the toolbar (**Figure 4.21**) and then choose *Files*. To place the cloud, tap *cloud* (**Figure 4.22**).

Figure 4.21 *Place Files.*   Figure 4.22 *Tap cloud.*

2. I think the size of the cloud is perfect. If you want to make it larger or smaller, drag the handles in the corners (**Figure 4.23**). Click *Done* when you're finished.

Figure 4.23 *Scale the cloud image, if necessary.*

3. Of course, we need to remove the background of this cloud. To do that, we start by making a selection. Long-press or double-tap the selection tools in the toolbar to reveal all selection tools.

4. Choose *Select Subject*. This option looks for the main object in the selected layer. In this case, that main object is easily identified, so Photoshop automatically selects the cloud (**Figure 4.24**). Magic!

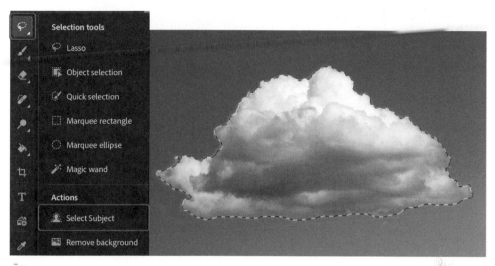

Figure 4.24 *Select Subject*

You may think that we're going to create a layer mask now, but we're not doing that yet. First, we'll make a small, but important improvement to the selection.

If we were to create a layer mask now, the edge of the cloud would be very hard, while outer edges of a cloud are usually very soft. We're therefore going to use the *Refine Edge* function. You may know this feature from the desktop version of Photoshop as part of Select and Mask. Actually, this function was originally intended for selecting hairs, but it works fine for a cloud too!

5. Now tap the *Refine Edge* button in the *Selection Properties bar*. (**Figure 4.25**).

 Figure 4.25 Refine Edge button

6. You now enter the *Refine Edge* workspace. To better see what you're doing, first set *View Mode* to *Overlay*. Everything that's not selected now turns red, and everything that is selected looks normal (**Figure 4.26**). You can see that the edges are still quite hard.

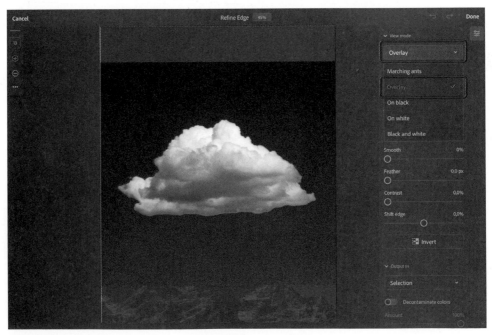

Figure 4.26 Set View Mode to Overlay.

7. First, we'll make the brush we're going to draw with a little larger. Do this by dragging the Brush Size slider upwards with your Apple Pencil or finger (**Figure 4.27**). Set the size to about 200 pixels.

8. Carefully draw along the edges of the cloud. Photoshop will recognize the "woolly edges" of the cloud as it would normally recognize hair and soften the mask edge for a more seamless transition. These edges also look a bit like hair, which is why it works so well. You can see the difference below in **Figure 4.28** (before) and **Figure 4.29** (after).

Figure 4.27

Set brush size.

Figure 4.28 Before Refine Edge

Figure 4.29 After Refine Edge

In most cases, you'd now be finished and could tap Done. But, you already feel it coming, there's still just a little too much blue reflection from the background along the edges of the cloud. As a result, the cloud will not blend nicely into the background. Photoshop can remove the color in these edges if you use *Decontaminate Colors*.

9. For this reason, turn on *Decontaminate Colors* in the *Output As* field. Because this function does destructive adjustments to the pixels of your layer, Photoshop automatically duplicates the layer to a new layer with a layer mask, to prevent you from accidentally ruining your original layer (**Figure 4.30**).

Figure 4.30 Decontaminate Colors

10. Now tap *Done*. You're back in the Edit workspace. Because you've chosen Decontaminate Colors, Photoshop has automatically created a new layer with layer mask. This makes the cloud transparent immediately and means you don't have to create the layer mask yourself. Note that there are now two cloud layers in the Layers panel: the original cloud layer, which has been made invisible, and a copy of it on which the layer mask has been applied (**Figure 4.31**).

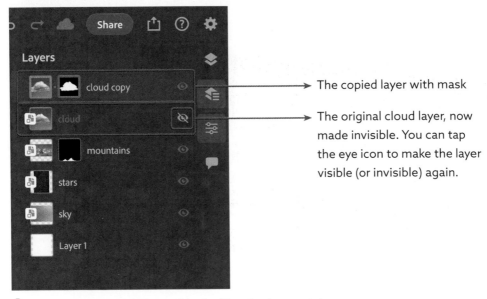

The copied layer with mask

The original cloud layer, now made invisible. You can tap the eye icon to make the layer visible (or invisible) again.

Figure 4.31 *A new masked copy of the cloud layer has been created*

Curves adjustment layer

Now the cloud is still a little too light. It would be nicer if the dark colors could be made a bit darker, and the light colors even more. We're therefore going to add a Curves adjustment layer so that we can control the exposure very precisely.

1. Make sure you still have the *cloud copy* layer selected in the Layers panel.
2. In the Layer Properties panel, tap *Add Clipped Adjustment* and choose *Curves* (**Figure 4.32**).

Figure 4.32 Add a clipped Curves adjustment layer.

3. As you read on page 26, a clipped adjustment layer is applied to only the next layer below it and not to all underlying layers. Notice that Photoshop added a new layer named Curves 1 to your layer stack. You can recognize a clipped adjustment layer by its arrow pointing directly to the underlying layer (**Figure 4.33**).

Figure 4.33 The little arrow next to the adjustment layer

Before we make any adjustments, you need to understand a bit more about how Curves work. You can set your iPad aside for now, but don't close the document. After a brief explanation in the next section, we'll continue where we just left off.

How do Curves work?

The moment you select a Curves adjustment layer, the Curves options appear in the Layer Properties panel (**Figure 4.34**). Curves always look very complicated at first, but once you learn how to work with them you'll see that it's not that difficult.

You'll see a diagonal line in this panel, with two little circles, called *nodes*, at the bottom left and top right. You can create as many nodes as you want by tapping on this diagonal line. And when you drag one of these nodes, you make an adjustment to the image, as the diagonal line becomes curved.

The little circle (or node) at the bottom left of the line controls the black point, the node at the top right controls the white point. One of the things you can do with these nodes is to change the overall contrast. If you move the black point to the right and the white point to the left, you improve the overall contrast. If you move the black point up and the white point down, you decrease the overall contrast.

If you place a node somewhere in the center of the line, you make the midtones lighter by dragging the node up and darker by dragging the node down.

Similarly, you can see that there is a graph of subtle lines in the Curves panel histogram. From the left, the three thicker vertical graph lines indicate the centers of the shadows, midtones, and highlights, respectively.

A little example: If you want to increase contrast, you actually want to make the shadows darker and the highlights lighter. In that case, you can create a node on the first vertical line (the shadows) and drag it down (make it darker). Then you create a node on the third vertical line and drag it up to lighten the light colors (**Figure 4.35**). And, because you can place nodes anywhere on the diagonal line, you have much more control over the contrast than with a Brightness/Contrast adjustment layer.

You can also lower the contrast by doing the opposite (**Figure 4.36**), or even adjust the color balance by tapping one of the colored dots (red, green or blue) and adjusting its curve (**Figure 4.37**).

TIP: When a node is selected, the Delete 🗑 icon becomes active under the graph. Tapping it deletes the node.

Midtones

Shadows Highlights

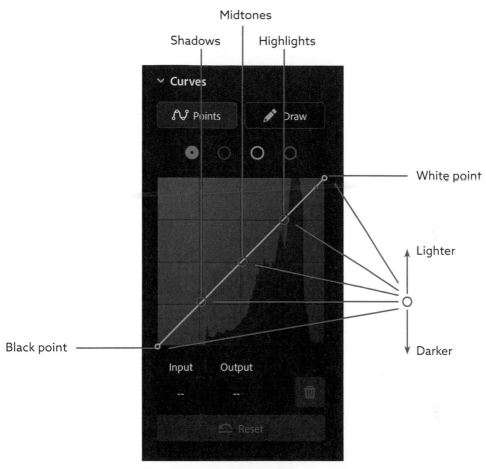

White point

Lighter

Darker

Black point

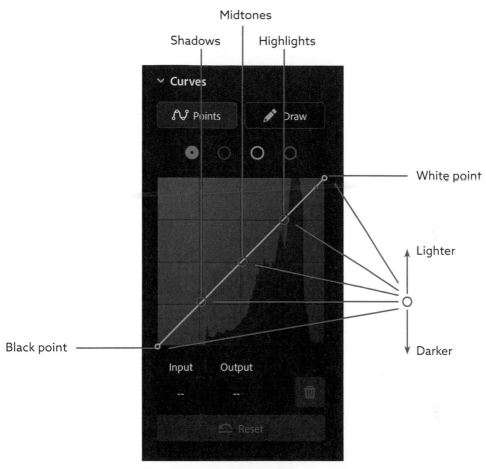

Figure 4.34 Curves

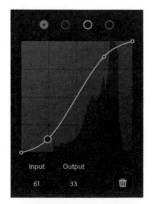

Figure 4.35 Increase contrast around the midtones.

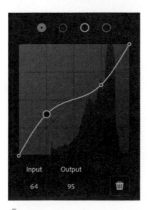

Figure 4.36 Decrease contrast around the midtones.

Figure 4.37 Red midtones lighter

With a better understanding of Curves, you can now get back to work. It's time to adjust the Curves layer we just created. The cloud is now too light everywhere, so we're going to darken both the light and dark colors.

1. Tap the Curves line to place a node—a small circle—in the shadow area and then drag it down slightly (**Figure 4.38**). Notice that the darker colors in the cloud get slightly darker.
2. Create a node in the highlights area, and drag it down slightly (**Figure 4.39**). The light colors in the cloud become slightly darker.
3. Drag the node at the top right down a bit so that you darken the whites as well (**Figure 4.40**).

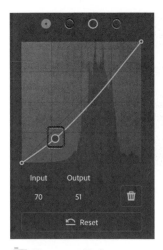

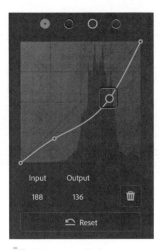

Figure 4.38 Node 1   Figure 4.39 Node 2   Figure 4.40 Node 3

4. Perfect! The cloud now looks darker and less contrasty (**Figure 4.41**). Do you think the dark colors could be made a little darker? Or the light colors a little lighter? If so, feel free to adjust the curve's nodes a little more.

Figure 4.41 The finished cloud

Object Selection tool

Time to place the lighthouse on the cloud! Again, we'll use similar techniques as in the previous exercises, but a little different so that you'll learn a couple of new things.

1. We'll start with placing an image again. Go to the *Place Photo* button in the toolbar, choose *Files* and place the image *lighthouse.jpg*.
2. The image is placed at exactly the right size. Tap *Done* when you're ready (**Figure 4.42**).

Figure 4.42 Place the lighthouse.

We'll make a selection around the lighthouse, but this time we'll use the *Object Selection tool* . This tool is one of the newer selection tools in the Photoshop ecosystem. You simply draw a rectangle around the object you want to select, then Photoshop searches for the subject within that selection. This is similar to *Select Subject*, but a little more bounded.

3. Activate the *Object Selection* tool by holding down the selection tools for a moment or by double-tapping it. The selection tools open so you can select the *Object Selection* tool (**Figure 4.43**).

Figure 4.43 *Object Selection tool*

4. Use this tool to draw a rectangle around the lighthouse (**Figure 4.44**). As soon as you release the stylus or your finger, Photoshop starts looking for the subject: the lighthouse (**Figure 4.45**).

Figure 4.44 *Drag a rectangle.*   Figure 4.45 *Object selected.*

The selection is almost perfect, but not quite yet. I would normally leave the selection as is, create a mask and then adjust the mask. But, on this selection, the *Refine Edge* feature from the previous exercise works very well too. Even though there is no hair present in this photo, Photoshop is still good at recognizing the thin elements around the lighthouse lamp.

5. Therefore, tap the *Refine Edge* button again in the *Active Selection Properties* bar at the bottom of the screen (**Figure 4.46**).

Figure 4.46 Refine Edge

6. You're back in the *Refine Edge* workspace (**Figure 4.47**). Because we set *View Mode* on the right side to *Overlay* in the previous exercise, it's probably still set this way. That's why the background is still red. If View Mode isn't set to Overlay, you can do that now. You can clearly see that the top part of the lighthouse isn't selected properly yet.

Figure 4.47 Make sure Overlay View mode is active.

7. Before drawing, make the brush slightly smaller (**Figure 4.48**) and set it to about *32 pixels*.

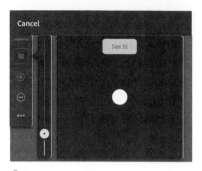

Figure 4.48 Change brush size.

8. Carefully draw over the white parts at the top of the lighthouse that should become transparent. It's not a big deal if the lines from the Refine Edge Brush aren't solid; they can look a little fuzzy. If you accidentally painted somewhere, in the tool options you can put the Refine Edge Brush in Subtract mode ⊖ to undo that. If you're happy with the end result, tap *Done*. Your selection now looks much better (**Figure 4.49**)!

9. Tap the *Mask* button in the *Active Selection Properties* bar which will create a layer mask. This'll make everything outside the selection transparent (**Figure 4.50**).

📷 *Figure 4.49 The selection*   📷 *Figure 4.50 Create a layer mask.*

Figure 4.51 Reposition the lighthouse.

10. Select the *Move* tool in the toolbar ▶ . Once that tool is selected, move the lighthouse up a bit so that it's positioned correctly (**Figure 4.51**).

11. The only drawback now is that the lighthouse is still in front of the cloud. In other words, it covers the cloud. To change that, drag the lighthouse layer in the Layers panel below the cloud copy layer. To do so, tap and hold the layer in the Layers panel and then drag it down until it's underneath the cloud copy layer (**Figure 4.52**). By the way, have you noticed the black-and-white mask added to the lighthouse layer?

That looks much better (**Figure 4.53**)! The lighthouse is now positioned behind the cloud. It's time to turn on the light of the lighthouse in the next exercise.

Figure 4.52 Drag the layer.

Figure 4.53 The lighthouse is now placed behind the cloud.

Drawing light with brushes and selections

Of course, a lighthouse without light is unacceptable. Therefore, in this exercise we'll draw the light ourselves in the photo composition.

1. First, make sure that the lighthouse layer is selected in the Layers panel. In step 2 we'll create a new empty layer, and it'll then be automatically placed on top of the lighthouse.
2. Now tap the ⊞ icon on the right side of the screen in the taskbar (**Figure 4.54**). This icon allows you to create new layers, groups and adjustment layers. Tap *New Layer*.
3. The new layer has been created, but is now called Layer 2 (**Figure 4.55**). Double-tap the layer name to rename it. Name the layer *Lamp*.

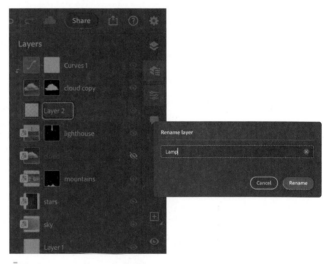

Figure 4.54 Add a new layer.   Figure 4.55 Rename the layer.

4. Select the *Brush* tool in the toolbar and increase the brush size to about *200 pixels*. A little larger or smaller is fine as well (**Figure 4.56**).
5. Now make the brush color yellow. You can do this by tapping on the topmost color chip (the foreground color) in the Tool Options, just above the brush size box (**Figure 4.57**).

6. I set the color to #FFF8E8. You can enter that color value in the HEX field (**Figure 4.57**). Alternatively, you can choose another hue in the color bar 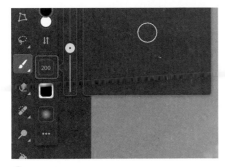 and then set the brightness of that hue in the square field above it. This works similar to the Color Picker in Photoshop on the desktop.

Figure 4.56 Increase the brush size.

Figure 4.57 Set the color to yellow.

7. Make sure the *Hardness* of the brush is set to 0%. Control this at the bottom of the Brush Tool Options (**Figure 4.58**).
8. Now with your finger or Apple Pencil, tap the top of the lighthouse. You'll immediately see a soft dot (**Figure 4.59**). Not satisfied? Then undo the step with a two-finger tap and start over. You can also tap two or three times in a row, or tap and hold your brush to paint a larger dot.

Figure 4.58
Brush hardness

Figure 4.59 Paint a light.

9. To blend the lamp light into the lighthouse a little better, we'll apply a blend mode again. In the *Layer Properties* panel, tap the *Blend Mode* list and select *Linear Dodge (Add)* (**Figure 4.60**). This blend mode makes the base layer (the lighthouse) brighter based on the color of our top layer (the lamp we just drew).

10. The lamp now blends better, but is still a little too bright. Move the *Opacity* slider to about 90% to make the lamp a little more transparent (**Figure 4.61**).

Figure 4.60 *Linear Dodge (Add).*   Figure 4.61 *Set the Opacity.*

That looks great! Now we'll create a beam of light using a new layer and the Lasso tool. I must admit that this is not the most convenient way, because at the time of writing this book, the Lasso tool does not yet have an option to draw straight lines. Adobe Fresco can already do this, so I expect that the Lasso tool will also become a combination of the Polygonal Lasso tool (which draws straight lines) and the "regular" Lasso in Photoshop as well. This will allow you to draw both straight (tap from point to point) and curved lines (drag) with the same tool.

11. Make sure the Lamp layer is selected in the Layers panel. The new layer in the next step will then be placed on top of it.

12. In the taskbar on the right side of the screen, tap the 🔳 icon and then tap *New Layer*.

13. Double-tap the layer name in the Layers panel to rename it. Name the layer *Beam*.

14. Now activate the *Lasso tool* ⌇ in the toolbar. If you don't see the Lasso tool, you may need to first tap and hold or double-tap the selection tool that is currently active to expand the various selection tools (**Figure 4.62**).

15. Use the *Lasso tool* to draw the selection you see in **Figure 4.62**. As mentioned, this is not very ideal because we can't draw straight lines at the moment, but the selection doesn't have to be perfect.

📷 *Figure 4.62 Draw a selection with the Lasso tool.*

16. Now select the *Paint Bucket* tool in the toolbar. With this bucket we're going to fill the selection. Make sure you've selected the same color as for the lamp (**Figure 4.63**). You can check the color by tapping the topmost color chip—the Foreground Color—at the bottom of the toolbar. (The color I used is, again #FFF8E8.)

17. Tap with the bucket in the middle of the selection to fill it with your chosen color (**Figure 4.64**).

18. We don't need the selection anymore, so you can now tap *Deselect* in the *Active Selection Properties* bar at the bottom of the screen (**Figure 4.64**).

Figure 4.63 *Set the color.*   Figure 4.64 *Deselect.*

19. The edge of the light beam is very hard. We'll therefore blur it with *Gaussian Blur*. In the taskbar on the right, tap the lightning icon ⚡, *Filters and Adjustments*. Tap *Gaussian Blur* (**Figure 4.65**).

Figure 4.65 *Gaussian Blur*

You're now in the *Gaussian Blur* workspace. Gaussian Blur is often used to blur images, but can also be used, for example, to soften the edges of a layer.

20. Set the *Blur Amount* to about *50* (**Figure 4.66**). You can see that the light beam becomes beautifully soft.

Figure 4.66 Change the Blur Amount.

21. Tap *Done* when you're finished.

Now, as with the lamp, we'll adjust the blend mode and transparency to ensure that the light beam blends nicely into the background.

22. In the *Blend Mode* list in the Layer Properties panel, choose *Linear Dodge (Add)* (**Figure 4.67**) and then change the *Opacity* to about *50%* (**Figure 4.68**). That looks great!

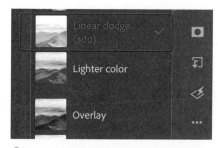

Figure 4.67 Blend mode

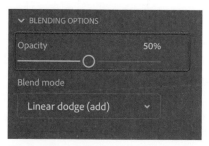

Figure 4.68 Opacity

Make whites transparent with blend modes

Our next component in the photo composition will be the rope ladder dangling at the bottom of the cloud. You'll notice that this image still has a white background, but we can easily remove that with a blend mode.

1. With the Beam layer selected in the Layers panel, tap the *Place Photo* button in the toolbar again and choose *Files*.
2. Select *ladder.jpg*.
3. Make the image slightly smaller and position it at the bottom of the cloud (**Figure 4.69**). If you don't see the ladder because it's hidden behind the cloud, that's not a problem. You can still move it around and make it smaller.
4. Tap *Done* when you're finished.

Figure 4.69 Place and position the ladder.

5. In the *Layer Properties* panel, tap the list under *Blend mode* and choose *Multiply* (**Figure 4.70**). All the white colors disappear, because Multiply causes colors from the top layer to blend nicely with the colors from the layer below. Whites will be completely transparent, black stays black, and all the midtones darken the underlying layer.

This is already starting to look like something! In the next exercise, we'll place the fisherman on top of the cloud.

📷 *Figure 4.70 Apply the Multiply blend mode.*

Adjusting a mask with brushes

In this exercise we'll place the fisherman sitting on top of the cloud. At first, the steps are more or less the same as in the previous exercises: Place an image, make a selection and then create the mask to remove a background. In this case, however, it's almost impossible to get the selection perfect all at once. So, we'll have to make some adjustments in the mask afterwards to make the fishing rod look right. Here we go!

1. In the previous exercise, we ended with the ladder. Make sure you still have that layer selected in the Layers panel. The fisherman will then automatically appear on top of it, and therefore behind the cloud.

2. Tap the *Place Photo* button, choose *Files* and select the image *fisherman*.

3. The image is placed behind the cloud, so drag it down a bit if necessary (**Figure 4.71**).

4. You can see that the fisherman is now looking in the wrong direction. At the upper right of the workspace you'll find two transformation buttons that allow you to flip an image (**Figure 4.72**). Tap the right mirror button: *Flip Horizontal* ⬥. The fisherman is now looking in the right direction.

Figure 4.71 *Place the fisherman.*

Figure 4.72 *Flip Horizontal*

5. Tap *Done* to return to the Edit workspace.

TIP: If you accidentally tapped Done too soon, you can always return to the Transform workspace by tapping the Transform button in the toolbar (**Figure 4.73**) or by simply dragging one of the transform handles if you have Auto-Select Layer on Canvas enabled in the Move tool settings (you probably have). You can resize, skew, distort or reflect the selected layer in the Transform workspace, just like you did when you first placed the image.

Figure 4.73

Transform tool

6. Select the *Object Selection* tool in the toolbar (**Figure 4.74**).

With the Object Selection tool, by default, you draw a rectangle around the object you want to select. Photoshop then searches for the main object within that selection. In this case, it might be better to draw a lasso around the fisherman, because you can select even more precisely then.

7. Tap the three dots (More Options) in the Tool Options panel (**Figure 4.75**). Under *Style*, Rectangle is selected now. Tap *Rectangle* to collapse the list and switch to *Lasso*.

Figure 4.74 Object Selection tool

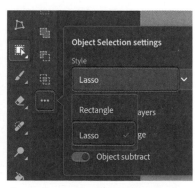

Figure 4.75 Lasso Object Selection

8. Carefully draw a lasso selection around the fisherman (**Figure 4.76**). This doesn't have to be very precise; you may draw around it quite widely. Photoshop will start looking for the subject anyway after you release your stylus.

Figure 4.76 Drag a lasso around the fisherman.

9. Release your Pencil, and your selection should then look similar to **Figure 4.77**.

Figure 4.77 Fisherman selected!

10. Tap the *Mask* button in the Active Selection Properties bar at the bottom of your screen (**Figure 4.78**).

Figure 4.78 Tap the Mask button.

Photoshop made the layer mask, but it doesn't look perfect yet. We are still missing a piece of the fishing rod.

Modifying a layer mask

As you remember from our layer mask discussion on page 28, white areas reveal the layer underneath the mask. So, **Figure 4.79** tells us the fisherman will be visible, but his fishing rod will not. Time to get to work.

If you want to modify a mask, you first need to tap the layer mask square in the Layers panel. When the layer mask is active, a blue border will appear around it. You can then start drawing with a brush on the canvas. If you want to hide more areas, paint with black; if you want to restore masked areas, paint with white. If you want partial transparency, paint with a shade of gray. You can repeat this process as many times as you like, until you're completely happy with the end result.

1. Tap the layer mask of the fisherman layer in the Layers panel (**Figure 4.79**). We can now start working in the mask.

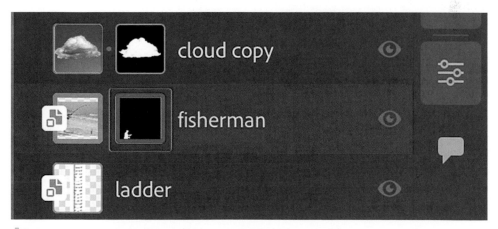

Figure 4.79 *Select the layer mask in the Layers panel.*

2. Select the *Brush* tool in the toolbar. We'll reveal the rod in a moment, so the brush shouldn't be too large. Set it to about *55 pixels* (**Figure 4.80**).

3. Set the hardness of the brush to about 60%. You can set the brush hardness at the bottom of the brush options, just like when we drew the lighthouse lamp.

It's important that you start drawing with a white brush, because you're going to reveal the rod. Once you tap on the fisherman layer mask in the Layers panel, the two color chips at the top of your Brush Options panel will automatically become black and white (**Figure 4.81**). You can easily switch these colors by dragging the top color chip down. This is handy because it allows you to quickly switch between black and white. You can also tap the color switch button just below the two color chips.

4. Now make sure the top color is white.

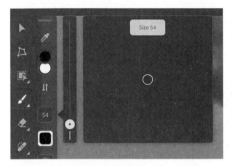

Figure 4.80 Set the brush size.

Figure 4.81 Switch colors.

5. For easier drawing, I turn the canvas on its side and zoom in a bit. You can zoom in by pinching with two fingers. Pinching outwards is zooming in, inwards is zooming out. If you simultaneously rotate your hand while pinching, the canvas rotates as well (**Figure 4.82**). Zoom and rotate the canvas now.

6. Draw with the white brush over the approximate location of the rod. It doesn't matter if you also reveal some of the surrounding image. That's what happened to me, as you can see in **Figure 4.82**. In fact, this "drawing too much" is very useful, because then we know exactly how much to take away again in the next step.

7. When the rod is visible, change the color to black by dragging the white color chip down in the Brush Options panel. Now

carefully draw along the edge of the fishing rod to hide the overdrawn areas again (**Figure 4.83**).

Figure 4.82 Rotate the canvas.

8. Continue until you are completely satisfied (**Figure 4.84**).

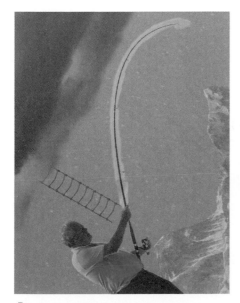

Figure 4.83 Paint in the layer mask.

Figure 4.84 Finished!

9. Rotate your canvas back to the original position by pinching with two fingers and rotating at the same time. When the canvas is rotated back to 0 degrees again, the canvas snaps to the original portrait position (**Figure 4.85**).

Figure 4.85 Return the canvas to its original portrait position.

Transform an object

The fisherman is still too large and is in the wrong position. Let's give him a lift into the cloud.

1. Tap the *Move* tool and tap the fisherman layer.
1. Tap one of the transformation handles on the canvas or tap the *Transform* tool (**Figure 4.86**) to go to the Transform workspace.
2. Drag one of the transformation handles to reduce the fisherman's size, and move him on top of the cloud (**Figure 4.87**).

Figure 4.86

Transform tool

TIP: If you want to rotate an object, drag the rotation handle (**Figure 4.87**).

3. Tap *Done* when you're finished.

📷 *Figure 4.87 Scale, position and, if necessary, rotate the fisherman.*

Drawing with a brush

All we're missing is a fishing line. Let's draw this line with a brush on a new layer.

1. In the taskbar on the right side of the screen, tap the ▦-icon and tap *New Layer*.
2. Rename the layer to *Fishing line* by double-tapping the layer name in the Layers panel.
3. Select the Brush tool 🖌 in the toolbar.
4. Change the foreground color (tap the top color chip in the Brush Options panel) to light gray. I used #A5A5A5 (**Figure 4.88**).
5. Change the brush size to about *12 pixels* (**Figure 4.89**).
6. Change the brush hardness to about *80%* (**Figure 4.90**).

📷 *Figure 4.88 Set the color.*

📷 *Figure 4.89 Resize the brush.*

📷 *Figure 4.90 Brush hardness*

7. Now, with a quick brush stroke, draw the fishing line as shown in **Figure 4.91**. If the line is not right, you can tap with two fingers to undo the last step and start over.

Figure 4.91 Draw the fishing line.

That looks fantastic!

Place photo and Remove Background

In the next steps, we'll place the fish, and you'll learn how to duplicate the an object and change its color.

1. Tap the *Place Photo* button, choose *Files* and select *fish*.
2. The fish is looking in the wrong direction, so tap the *Flip Horizontal* button (**Figure 4.92**). If you don't see the fish because it's hidden behind the cloud, that's not a problem. You can still move it around and flip it.

Figure 4.92 Reflect the fish.

3. Don't change the size of the fish yet. In the next step we'll remove the background, which works better and easier if the fish is larger. For now, tap *Done*.

You can remove the fish's background in several ways. One option is to first make a selection around the fish—with, for example, the Object Selection tool—and then create a layer mask. However, in cases where a subject is easily identified, you can also use the super-fast *Remove Background* feature.

4. Make sure the fish layer is selected in the Layers panel.
5. Tap and hold the active selection tool in the toolbar or tap it twice to collapse the selection tools. Now select *Remove Background* in the Actions section (**Figure 4.93**).

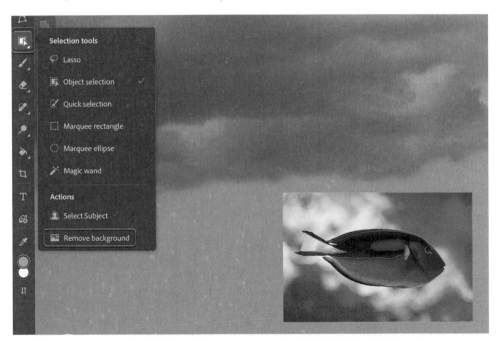

Figure 4.93 Tap Remove Background.

The nifty thing about Remove Background is that it removes the background by adding a layer mask. You can therefore easily adjust the transparency afterwards by activating the mask in the Layers panel and then drawing with a black or white brush. (**Figure 4.94**).

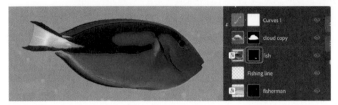

Figure 4.94 *A layer mask has been added.*

6. Select the fish in the Layers panel and tap the *Transform tool* or one of the on-canvas transform handles. Make the fish smaller (**Figure 4.95**).

Figure 4.95 *Make the fish smaller.*

7. Tap *Done* when you're finished.

In Photoshop on the desktop, you can use the Move tool to move an object. If you press Alt (or Option in macOS) before moving and hold it while moving, the object is duplicated. In Photoshop on the iPad, you can tap and hold the secondary touch shortcut instead. (You can read all about the touch shortcut on page 33).

8. Activate the Move tool ▶. Make sure the fish layer is still active in the Layers panel.

9. Before you start moving the fish, tap and hold the secondary touch shortcut: Tap and hold the center of the touch shortcut with your finger, then drag your finger to the outer edge of the touch shortcut. Also note the blue Duplicate tool tip in the upper-right corner of the screen. While holding the secondary touch shortcut, move the fish. It will now be duplicated. Do that twice so that you have three fish (**Figure 4.96**).

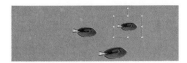 Figure 4.96 Tap and hold the secondary touch shortcut to duplicate the fish.

10. The three fish now all look the same. Therefore, we're going to transform the two copied fish a bit. To do so, tap a fish layer in the Layers panel or on canvas, scale the fish down— you now know how to do that!—and tap *Done* (**Figure 4.97**).

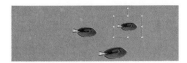 Figure 4.97 Scale the fish to different sizes.

11. Now select the *fish copy* layer. Scale the fish down and rotate it a little via the rotation handle (**Figure 4.98**). Tap *Done* when you're finished.

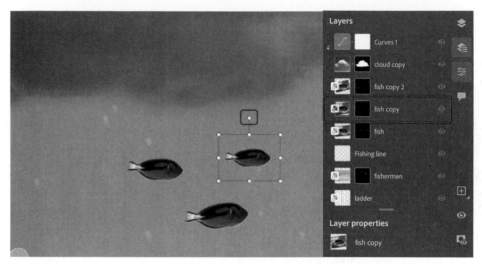

Figure 4.98 Rotate the fish.

Now that the fish are looking as realistic as they can while floading in midair, we'll group them. In a layer group, layers are still selectable individually, but your Layers panel looks a lot more organized. One of the other advantages of layer groups is that you can apply a clipped adjustment layer to the entire group, meaning, for example, you can change the color of all the fish at once.

12. To group layers, you first have to select them. Tap and hold the primary touch shortcut (**Figure 4.99**, Step A).
13. Select the three layers in the Layers panel by tapping them one at a time (**Figure 4.99**, Step B).
14. When the three fish layers are selected, tap the *Group Layers* icon ▢ in the taskbar on the right side of the screen (**Figure 4.99**, Step C). The layers are now grouped (**Figure 4.100**).
15. Double-tap the group name in the Layers panel, and rename the group *Fish* (**Figure 4.101**).

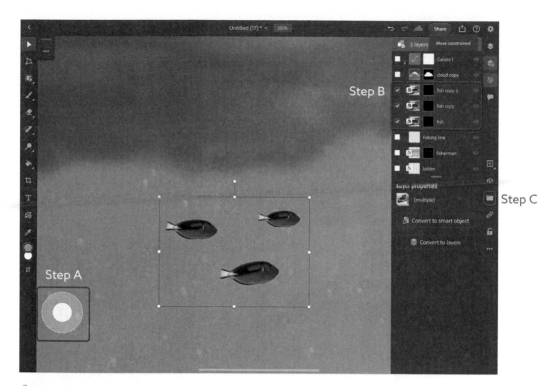

Figure 4.99 *Select multiple layers and make a layer group.*

Figure 4.100 *Double-tap the group name.*

Figure 4.101 *Rename the layer group.*

Changing colors with Hue/Saturation

With all the fish layers in a group, we can change the color of all the fish at the same time using a clipped adjustment layer. "Clipped" means that the adjustment layer is applied only to the layer or group directly below it and not to all the other underlying layers. We combined a clipped adjustment layer with Curves to darken the cloud earlier in the chapter. This time we'll use a clipped *Hue/Saturation* adjustment layer, which lets you to control the hue, saturation and lightness of a layer or layer group.

1. Make sure the *Fish* group is selected in the Layers panel.
2. Tap the three dots at the bottom of the taskbar, and tap *Add Clipped Adjustment* (**Figure 4.102**). In the Add Clipped Adjustment panel, choose *Hue/Saturation*.
3. After Photoshop adds the Hue/Saturation adjustment layer to the Layers panel, notice that the settings appear in the Layer Properties panel (**Figure 4.103**).

Figure 4.102 Add a clipped adjustment layer.

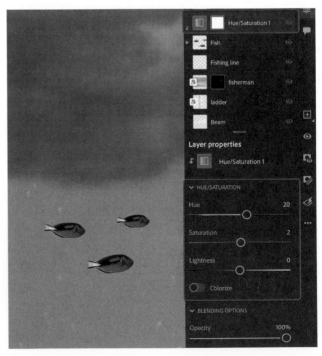

Figure 4.103 Hue/Saturation adjustment layer

When you drag the *Hue* slider, all the colors in the underlying layer or layer group shift toward a different color in the color spectrum. In **Figure 4.103**, you can see that Hue is moved to the right, toward 28 degrees. That means that all colors are shifted sideways by 28 degrees toward another color in the color circle. That color circle is no longer a circle in the Hue bar, but displayed horizontally. As you can see, the ends on the left and right both end up in red. In a circle, they would match up nicely.

If you drag the Hue slider to the right, red becomes orange/yellow and blue becomes magenta/purple. That way, you can easily change colors of objects.

Furthermore, you can adjust the *Saturation* slider, which controls the saturation or intensity of a color. The further you shift Saturation to the right, the more saturated the colors become. If you shift Saturation to the left, all color gradually disappears from your image until it's black and white. I set Saturation to 2, because the colors were already quite saturated.

4. Now play with the *Hue/Saturation* sliders yourself until you're happy with the result.

Wow, these were quite a lot of steps, but your first Photoshop on iPad photo composition is finished! There are a few more things I want to show you, though. For example, you'll probably want to share your composition with someone else, or maybe even continue working in Photoshop on the desktop. In the Extra section of this chapter, you'll see how to import brushes and how to further edit the composition in Lightroom for mobile for a few final general color edits.

Save and share files

There are several ways you can save or share a file, which you'll see in the following sections.

Photoshop Cloud Documents

Your file is automatically saved as a Photoshop Cloud Document (a *PSDC* file) every few minutes. You don't have to do anything for that.

You can also manually save edits by tapping the file name in the top center of the Photoshop on the iPad Edit workspace (**Figure 4.104**), then tapping Save Now. This is a good way to ensure all your recent edits are saved before, for example, switching to Photoshop on the desktop for further work on the file (more on this shortly).

NOTE: Because you can't work in Photoshop on the iPad and Photoshop on the desktop at the same time, you need to close the opened document first by returning to the Photoshop Home screen. To do this, tap the arrow ◄ at the upper left of the screen.

📷 *Figure 4.104 Force Photoshop to save your Cloud Document.*

Rename your file

By default, a Photoshop Cloud Document is called "Untitled (number)." Therefore, it's always advisable to change the document name, otherwise you'll quickly lose track of all your documents. Here's a quick guide to renaming files:

IN THE EDIT WORKSPACE Tap the file name at the top center of the Edit workspace (**Figure 4.104**). Then tap the file name listed below it, next to the document thumbnail. A popup appears where you can edit the file name (**Figure 4.105**). Rename the file and tap *Rename*.

IN THE PHOTOSHOP HOME SCREEN If you leave the document by tapping the arrow ◀ in the upper-left corner of the Edit workspace, you'll return to the Home screen. If you tap the three dots at the bottom of the document thumbnail there, you can rename the file by tapping *Rename* (**Figure 4.106**).

Try it now, and rename your document to *Photoshop lighthouse comp*.

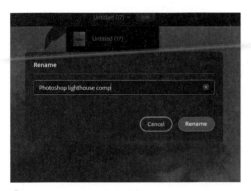

📷 *Figure 4.105 Rename your Cloud Document.* 📷 *Figure 4.106 Rename in the Home screen.*

IN THE CREATIVE CLOUD APP If you've installed the Creative Cloud app, you can also rename the file there by tapping the three dots at the bottom of the document thumbnail in the Home screen (**Figure 4.107**) or in the Files section.

📷 *Figure 4.107 Rename a file in the Creative Cloud app.*

Continuous editing between the iPad and desktop

As soon as you open Photoshop on the desktop, you will find your
iPad Cloud Document directly in the Home screen (**Figure 4.108**).
If you click on it, the document will download and open. You can
then continue working on the desktop. All layers are there, so
you have access to maximum editing capabilities. Features not
yet available on the iPad, but available on the desktop, can still be
applied to the document this way. If you don't see your document in
the Home screen, you can find it under Your Files on the left side of
the screen (**Figure 4.108**).

The great thing is that this document also remains saved as a Cloud
Document. When you restart Photoshop on the iPad, the document
there will be updated with all the changes you made on the
desktop. You can keep switching back and forth between iPad and
desktop until your document is finished.

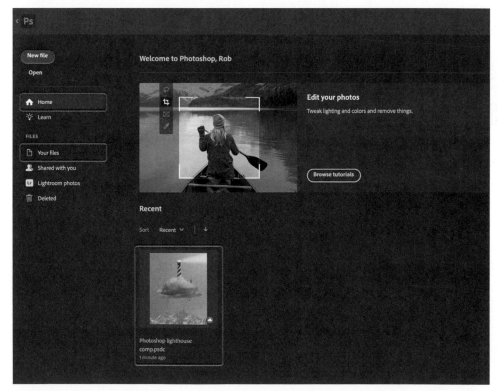

Figure 4.108 Open your Photoshop Cloud Document in Photoshop on the desktop.

Exporting your file

If you want to share a document or simply save it as a JPG on your iPad, you can do so using the Export icon ⬆ in the upper-right corner of the Edit workspace (**Figure 4.109**).

The most versatile option is *Publish and Export* (**Figure 4.109**). Once you tap on it you'll see the options shown in **Figure 4.110**. You can choose from the following file formats:

PNG: Useful for saving and sharing images. It preserves transparency.
JPG: Commonly used for showing photos on web sites, and sharing photos on email or social media. Quality is set to 8 by default. The lower you set the quality, the blockier and worse the quality of your JPG. But, the file size does get smaller and smaller too. I usually find 8 to be a good choice for online sharing. A setting above 8 doesn't have much better quality, while the file size goes up considerably.
PSD: Useful for when you want to save a copy of your Cloud Document as a "regular" Photoshop document (PSD) on your iPad or in an online storage space. I usually use this format when backing up.
TIFF: Can preserve more original quality than JPEG because TIFF uses lossless compression, while JPEG uses lossy compression. In Photoshop on the iPad, a TIFF is saved with all its layers, so if you open it with Photoshop, you can edit all those layers as well. I almost never use TIFF anymore, because PSD or JPG are usually great alternatives.

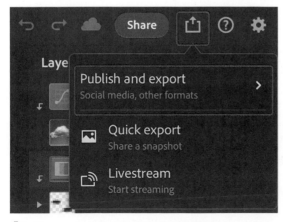

Figure 4.109 Choose Publish and Export.

Figure 4.110 File formats

When you tap the *Export* button (at the bottom of **Figure 4.110**), you'll be given a number of choices about where to export the document (**Figure 4.111**). The choices you get here depend on the apps you've installed on your iPad and some other iPad settings. The options you're most likely to use are:

Save Image: Saves your photo in the native iPad Photos app.

Save to Files: Saves to your iPad Files app. You can also access any cloud services linked to your iPad, such as Creative Cloud or Dropbox there. Useful if you want to back up the PSD file.

Lightroom: Exports your image to Lightroom. You'll see this app in the top row only if Lightroom is installed on your iPad. Exporting your image to Lightroom is very useful if you want to do some global, final color and exposure edits to your complete Photoshop document.

Mail: Attaches the image file to a new message in the Apple Mail app. This is useful if you want to email the file directly to someone via the Apple Mail app.

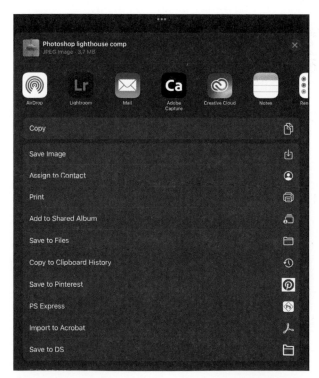

Figure 4.111 *Choices about where to export your document*

Quick Export

In **Figure 4.109**, you also see the *Quick Export* option. That feature is not really different from Publish and Export, except that you no longer get the choice of which file type to save.

Quick Export always exports a JPG. You immediately get the same list of export options seen in **Figure 4.111**, so you can export that JPG file directly to your chosen medium. I usually choose Publish and Export instead of Quick Export, because I prefer to have control over the final file format.

Livestream

If you have a Behance account and you want to start a livestream directly from Photoshop on the iPad, you can. Tap the *Livestream* button (**Figure 4.112**) to start a stream on portfolio website **Behance.net**. Your Behance followers can then immediately see how you create a composition in Photoshop on the iPad or how you edit a photo. Your iPad webcam is also shared, so you are in the picture too. The livestream can also be watched later and shared on Behance.

Figure 4.112 Livestream in Photoshop

Invite to edit and invite for review

At the top of the Photoshop screen, you will also find a blue Share button
`Share`. This button allows you to invite people so they can also work and/or
comment on this Photoshop document.

Once you tap the Share button, you will be taken to a Share Document
window (**Figure 4.113**), where you can enter the email address of the
person you want to invite. By tapping the gear icon, you can also set
whether only invited people or anyone with the link can view the file, if
comments are allowed or if someone can also save a copy of the file (**Figure
4.114**).

If the invited email address is also associated with a Creative Cloud or
Photoshop subscription, the person you invite will receive an email with
the invitation *and* a notification in the Creative Cloud app. After they click
on the invitation, they can edit the file and comment on it in Photoshop on
the Web (**Figure 4.115**), iPad or desktop.

If no subscription is associated with the email address, the person
being invited will receive an invitation email only. After clicking on the
invitation, they can view the document and comment on it in Photoshop
on the Web.

NOTE: You cannot (yet) work on the document simultaneously and see
each other's changes immediately.

Figure 4.113 Share Document window   Figure 4.114 Share Document settings

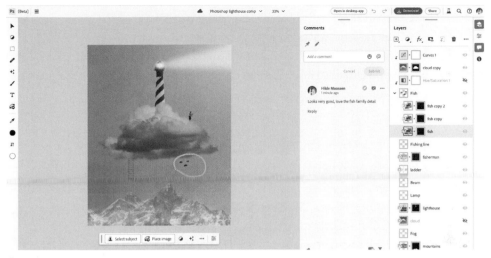

Figure 4.115 Invited people can edit and comment in Photoshop on the Web.

You can view and reply to the comments someone made on your Photoshop document in Photoshop on the iPad if you open the document and go to the *Comments* panel (**Figure 4.116**). You can also do this in Photoshop on the Web, desktop and the Creative Cloud app.

If a file has been shared with you, you can always find it in the Shared with You section in the Photoshop Home screen (**Figure 4.117**), in the Creative Cloud app and in Creative Cloud on the web.

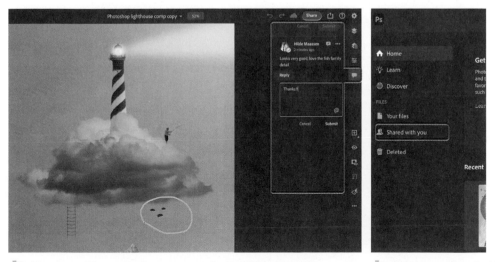

Figure 4.116 View and reply to comments in the Comments panel.

Figure 4.117 Shared with You

Version history

When Photoshop on the iPad saves your Cloud Document every few minutes, a version history is also maintained. With that version history, you can always go back to an earlier version of the document from up to 30 days back. This is useful if after a while you find that the version from two days earlier was better after all. A kind of 30-day Undo option, so to speak. Very useful!

You can view the version history if you tap the three dots next to the file name in the Photoshop Home screen (**Figure 4.118**). Then choose View Version History. The Version History window appears (**Figure 4.119**). On the right side of the screen you can browse through and tap the saved versions to view them. When you find a version you want to revert, tap the three dots next to the specified time and choose Revert to This Version (**Figure 4.120**). The document is reverted to that version then.

If you want to keep a version longer than 30 days, you can do so by tapping the Marker icon next to the corresponding version. This version will then be saved in the Marked Versions section. You can always revert to that version there.

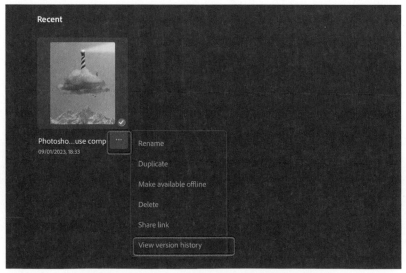

Figure 4.118 View Version History of a Photoshop Cloud Document

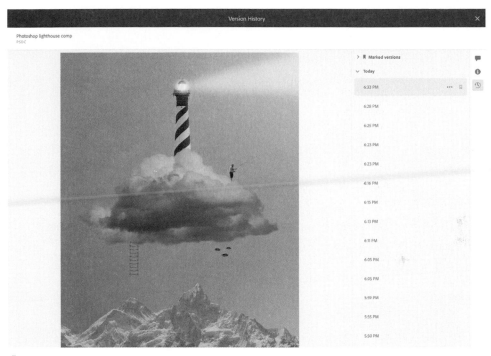

Figure 4.119 The Version History window

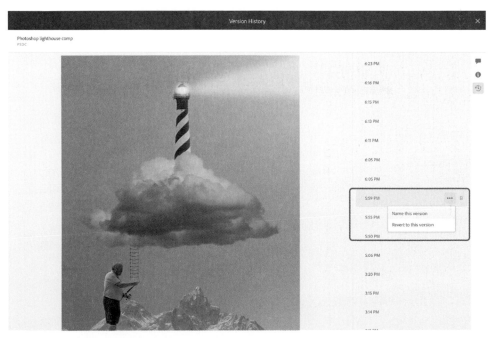

Figure 4.120 Revert to This Version

Extra: Import and paint with brushes

Here's a cool thing: You can import brushes (ABR files) into Photoshop on the iPad, whether you made them yourself or purchased them. Plus, from Adobe's website you can download a lot of free brushes created by the famous brush maker Kyle Webster. These are fantastic brushes that allow you to paint with charcoal and different types of paint, as well as brushes that allow you to quickly draw hair, grass, clouds fog or leaves, to name just a few of the many possibilities. Here's how to try out both options. We'll start by importing and drawing with a brush I pre-made in Photoshop on the desktop.

Import a cloud brush

If you want to import a brush, you can follow these steps:

1. Make sure you've still got your lighthouse composition open.
2. Double-tap the *Brush* tool in the toolbar to open the Brushes panel.
3. At the bottom of this panel, tap the + icon.
4. Choose *Import from Files* (**Figure 4.121**).
5. Find the exercise folder for this chapter on your iPad or online storage, and navigate to the *Brushes* folder. Tap *cloud-brush.abr*, which is the brush I created in Photoshop on the desktop (**Figure 4.122**).

The brush is now loaded into your Brushes panel. This panel automatically scrolls all the way down, where you'll see a folder containing the Cloud Brush.

Figure 4.121 Import and discover brushes

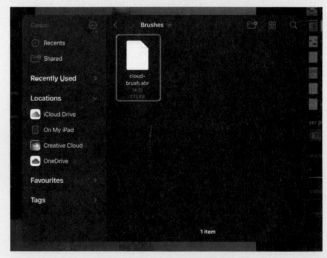

Figure 4.122 Import cloud-brush.abr

6. Tap the *cloud-brush* folder in the Brushes panel (**Figure 1.123**).
7. And now tap the *Cloud Brush* (**Figure 1.124**).

Before we can start painting with the Cloud Brush, we'll first create a new layer.

8. Select the *Mountains layer* in the Layers panel
9. Tap the 🔲 icon in the taskbar, and tap *New layer*.
10. The new layer has been created, but is now called *Layer 2* or something similar. Double-tap the layer name to rename it. Name the layer *Fog*.
11. If necessary, resize your brush to something between 400 and 500 pixels in the Brush settings (**Figure 4.125**).

Figure 4.123 Brush folder   Figure 4.124 Tap Cloud Brush.   Figure 4.125 Resize the brush.

12. Start painting with your Fog brush, on top of the mountains.

TIP: An incredibly useful feature is that you can also press the primary touch shortcut while drawing (**Figure 4.126**). Your brush then automatically switches to an eraser of the same brush type (in this case, the Cloud Brush). So you can very easily paint with Fog, erase with Fog, draw and erase again until you are completely happy and satisfied.

Figure 4.126 Erase while tapping and holding the primary touch shortcut.

13. The clouds on the mountains may be a little too present now. If necessary, lower the Fog layer's *Opacity* in the Layer Properties panel (**Figure 4.127**).

Figure 4.127 Lower the Opacity of the Fog layer.

The end result now looks even cooler than before (**Figure 4.128**). On the next page, let's have a look at how to download even more free, premium brushes from the Adobe website.

Figure 4.128 *The end result after painting with the Fog brush.*

Extra: Discover more brushes

You can download a lot of free brushes from Adobe's website, created by the famous brush maker Kyle Webster. These fantastically versatile brushes offer many creative possibilities. Here's a guide on how to download these premium brushes.

Import Kyle Webster brushes

If you want to import Kyle Webster's brushes, you can follow these steps:

1. Double-tap the *Brush* tool in the toolbar to open the Brushes panel.
2. At the bottom of this panel, tap the + icon.
3. Choose *Discover New Brushes* (**Figure 4.129**).
4. You'll be directed to Adobe's Download Exclusive Brushes page (**Figure 4.130**). If you're not signed in with your Adobe ID, sign in now.
5. You'll see a long list with all types of brushes here. Choose the brush package you would like and tap *Download*.

The file containing all the brushes will be downloaded. You can now choose to use Safari to open the downloaded file. The brushes are then likely to be opened in Photoshop and imported directly into the Brushes panel.

Figure 4.129 Discover brushes.

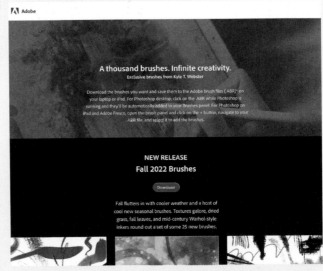

Figure 4.130 Download brushes from the Adobe website.

You can also save the downloaded file on your iPad, then go back to Photoshop, and open the Brushes panel again (**Figure 4.129**). If you tap on the + icon, choose *Import from Files*. You will then be taken to the Files app, where you can find your brush package, just like we did when we imported the Cloud Brush on the previous pages.

6. Once you have imported the brush package, tap the corresponding folder in the Brushes panel (*Fall-2022* in **Figure 1.131**).

7. Then tap the brush you want to paint with (**Figure 1.132**).

I recommend that you try out as many brushes as you can, and see what wonderful things are possible!

Figure 4.131 Brush folder

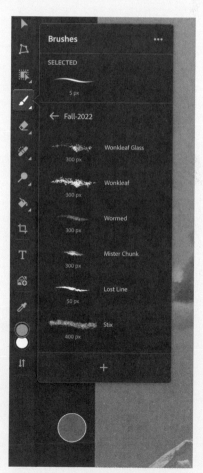

Figure 4.132 Choose brushes.

Extra: Editing in Lightroom

In the desktop version of Photoshop, I regularly use the Camera Raw Filter. This allows you to easily adjust exposure and color of the entire composition through one single filter. Think of it as final edit before saving the final composition. In Photoshop on the iPad, the Camera Raw Filter isn't available, but you can still apply the same edits, because you have access to Lightroom for mobile. In Lightroom, you can perform exactly the same operations as with Camera Raw Filter. Of course, it's important that you first download Lightroom from the Apple App Store. For the largest part, the app is free to use. If you have a paid Creative Cloud subscription, all features are included.

Export your composition to Lightroom

In the previous exercises, you read how to share and save your composition. Similarly, you can send the composition to Lightroom for final post-processing.

1. Make sure you have the composition open in Photoshop. Then tap the Export icon ⬆ and choose *Publish and Export* (**Figure 4.133**).
2. You can then choose a file format, such as JPG with quality 12. Of course, you may also choose PSD, in which case your entire Photoshop document will be sent to Lightroom. Tap *Export*.
3. Choose *Lightroom* (**Figure 4.134**).
4. Your photo will be sent to Lightroom. If Lightroom doesn't open automatically, open the app yourself.

Figure 4.133 Publish and Export

Figure 4.134 Export to Lightroom for mobile.

Once you've opened the photo in Lightroom, the screen looks like **Figure 4.135**. On the right, you'll see all the different tabs you can open to adjust the photo. If this is your first time opening Lightroom, the Light and Color sections are often more than enough to start with. But, it never hurts to look at the other sections as well. You can't do much wrong, because you can undo all the settings. In the worst case, you can just resend the photo from Photoshop to Lightroom again. Of course, this is not a Lightroom book, so I won't go into great detail about this app. But, feel free to explore. For instance, Lightroom is very handy on an iPad if you're traveling and want to quickly edit your photos, as Russell Brown will also show you in the next interview chapter.

The following steps show you how you could edit the image in Lightroom, and then save it to your iPad.

Figure 4.135 The Lightroom for mobile interface

1. First, change the exposure settings in the *Light* tab (**Figure 4.136**). For the example, I increased *Contrast* a little (+7), made the *Highlights* a little darker (–24) and made the *Shadows* a little lighter (+16). Feel free to adjust the photo as you like it.

2. Tap the *Color* tab (**Figure 4.137**) and adjust. I slightly increased the *Tint* (+10), *Vibrance* (+16) and *Saturation* (+3) of the colors.

3. Tap *Effects* (**Figure 4.138**) and find a look you like. I increased *Texture* (+27), and dragged *Vignette* down a little (–21) to add a dark, soft border (a vignette) around the image.

Figure 4.136 *Edit Light.*

Figure 4.137 *Edit Color.*

Figure 4.138 *Edit Effects.*

4. Finally, in the *Detail* tab, adjust the *Sharpening* (+40) of the composition (**Figure 4.139**), so that the photo becomes a little sharper.

Figure 4.139 Edit Detail.

5. After these adjustments, I think the composition is perfect. You can share the photo with others in several ways. Tap the *Share* button in the upper-right corner, and you'll see all the options (**Figure 4.140**). These options are very similar to the sharing options in Photoshop we covered before. For example, *Share to* gives you the same menu as Publish and Export in Photoshop, and *Export to Camera Roll* lets you save your photo to the iPad Photos app. Handy!

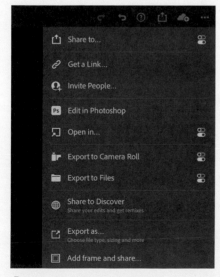
Figure 4.140 Share and export.

Figure 4.141 The end result

Chapter 5

Russell Brown

CREATIVE MOBILE PHOTOGRAPHY

Russell Brown is a Senior Creative Director at Adobe and an Emmy Award–winning instructor. He was introduced to Thomas and John Knoll, the original developers of Photoshop, when John Knoll gave him his first demo of Photoshop in 1989. Russell was instrumental in the development and launch of Photoshop 1.0. Most recently, he has been traveling the world with a smartphone camera to capture his adventures in an inspiring, creative way. He loves editing his images with Lightroom for mobile and Photoshop on the iPad and ultimately enjoys sharing his knowledge with others.

Name:	Russell Brown
Residence:	San Francisco, USA
Finds inspiration:	By following other photographers
Favorite tool:	Levels adjustments
Most used tools:	Levels, layers, compositing and masking
Other favorites:	Lightroom for mobile, Reflect Mirror Camera and Lenslight
Best advice:	Learn Photoshop like learning a new language: by doing it!

How do you work with Photoshop on the iPad?

I start shooting photos on my iPhone. It's fast, portable, takes great photos and you always have it with you. With each new iPhone model, the photo quality gets better and better. All the photos I capture are automatically sent to the Lightroom for mobile app on my iPhone, where I occasionally do some basic editing. But then I quickly continue editing on my iPad, because via Creative Cloud, Lightroom automatically syncs the photos to all my devices. I do most of the light and color edits in Lightroom on my iPad. I really like the large, intuitive screen. I don't even have a laptop anymore!

I then send my photo from Lightroom to Photoshop on the iPad, where I usually do different kinds of edits. Think of making composites, layering images and color editing with adjustment layers like Levels. In some cases, an image is great right away in Lightroom. Then I don't have to send it to Photoshop anymore.

Photoshop on the iPad is fantastic. I think I can do 90% of all my usual photo editing on the iPad. If I do need to make additional edits on the desktop, the whole Creative Cloud system allows me to do so very quickly.

© Russell Preston Brown

© Russell Preston Brown

What desktop features do you miss in Photoshop on the iPad?
I don't really need to do very advanced things on my iPad. But, for example, I'd love to have *Liquify*, which allows you to easily warp objects. More advanced blur functions and a sky replacement feature would also be great to have. It's likely that these features will be added later.

Also, in Photoshop on the desktop, I use *Channels* a lot. Those are not yet present on the iPad. Many of the things I do with Channels can also be done in other ways, but I'm someone from the early days of Photoshop and still like to use the old tools. I'm someone with bear skins and stone knives, haha! For example, I like to do color adjustments with *Levels*, while others use Color Balance for that.

Anyway, I find it super fun, inspiring and challenging that not all desktop features are present on the iPad. It makes you more creative and makes you approach things in a different way. Compare it to camping. At a campsite, you don't have a kitchen sink or stove. As a result, you may have to make a fire to boil an egg. But doesn't the boiled egg in the mobile kitchen taste much better than at home? That's how it is for me with Photoshop on the iPad and photography with a smartphone. I love challenges!

CHAPTER 5 | RUSSELL BROWN

Do you use the camera in the Lightroom for mobile app or the native iPhone camera app?

The Lightroom for mobile app has a really good camera. You probably expect me to use that camera, but I usually don't! I mostly use the iPhone's native camera. The reason is that in the native camera, Apple does magical things to the photo that aren't shared with the world. For example, if you accidentally move the camera a little while shooting and the photo is blurred, the software automatically takes out that blur, so the photo is sharp again. The Lightroom camera can't do that. Something similar is happening with colors in JPG processing. Apple doesn't share this magic with creators of other camera apps, making it basically impossible to get the same results. For the same reason, I use the native camera on almost all other smartphone brands like those from Google and Samsung.

Do you shoot your photos in raw?

I shoot my photos in raw and in JPG. Because of the magic that happens in JPG color processing in the native iPhone camera app, I end up using the JPG in certain cases. Especially with night photography. These magic JPG processes aren't applied to the raw photos and are almost impossible to

reproduce. You would expect to be able to reproduce all edits in a raw photo, but that isn't the case. Crazy but true!

Do you combine Photoshop and Lightroom with other apps?

There are so many great apps you can use to complement Photoshop and Lightroom! For example, I use *Reflect Mirror Camera*, which allows you to create reflections in water very quickly. I used Reflect Mirror Camera on a photo of a very famous tree in Arizona, to which I added a flood and a reflection. Anyone who knows that tree will know that there is no water nearby. But, it's art, and I really like this kind of editing.

Lenslight is also a very nice app that lets you quickly add light, lens flares and other effects. And, with the *Alien Sky* app I sometimes add celestial objects to photos. Usually these kinds of apps do things you can also do with Photoshop. That's why sometimes it feels a little like I'm cheating when I use an app like this. Especially since I've been associated with Photoshop and Adobe for so long, people expect me to do everything with Photoshop or Lightroom. However, most apps do one specific thing very quickly, and then it just saves me time. And of course, it's also really fun to try new things.

What type of iPad do you prefer?

The 10.5-inch iPad. I like to work very fast and mobile. Because of its smaller and more portable size, I find it easier to take this iPad with me. I also have a keyboard connected to it, because I use keyboard shortcuts in Photoshop a lot. And, of course, I also have an Apple Pencil.

Where do you get your inspiration?

I get inspired from books, magazines, videos, movies, Instagram, Facebook, as well as visiting galleries and museums. I'm a fan of photographers like Greg Gorman, Joel Grimes and Joe McNally. The ease of following photographers and artists on Instagram and Facebook is incredible. The nice thing is that they not only share their photos, but often their setups and the equipment they use. I get a lot of inspiration from that. And lately I've been crazy about shooting portraits. It's such a great way to learn about light and the process behind photography.

© Russell Preston Brown

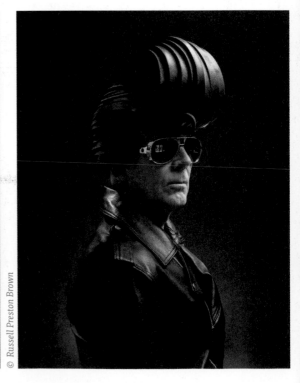

© Russell Preston Brown

© Russell Preston Brown

What new developments do you think are coming to Photoshop on the iPad in the near future?

Since all the code from Photoshop on the desktop is also used for Photoshop on the iPad, you can already guess a little by yourself which features will be coming to the iPad in the near future. Everything that most people like to use in Photoshop on the desktop will probably be activated one by one in the iPad version at some point. Think of Liquify and Sky Replacement.

Do you have any tips and tricks for Photoshop beginners?

I certainly have! You only learn Photoshop by doing it. Lock yourself up in a room, start creating projects in Photoshop, take a course or watch online tutorials. It's like learning a new language. You have to force yourself to actively speak that language and completely immerse yourself in it. It's exactly the same with learning Photoshop. Start with the basics and create your own projects. For example, first take two images and then task yourself with combining those images. That's the only way to master Photoshop. Just start doing it!

© Russell Preston Brown

© Russell Preston Brown

Chapter 6

Retouching

INTUITIVELY RETOUCH IMAGES

The Spot Healing Brush tool and the Clone Stamp tool are familiar tools in the desktop version of Photoshop. They allow you to easily remove blemishes and spots in photos. Because both tools are brushes, the iPad with an Apple Pencil is the ideal tool for retouching. This chapter shows you how to retouch intuitively and how to edit your raw photos in Lightroom and then post-process them in Photoshop on the iPad.

Retouching an old photo

With their spots and cracks, old photos make perfect subjects for demonstrating the Spot Healing Brush. For this exercise, we'll be using a photo of my dear grandfather from 1932, when he was eight years old. After removing the obvious blemishes, we'll go a step further by applying color corrections with Curves and Hue/Saturation adjustment layers.

The Spot Healing Brush is my most used retouching tool. With it, you draw over a spot or blemish. Then Photoshop extracts information from surrounding areas of the photo and intelligently places that information on top of the spot. In other words, the blemish isn't actually removed, but other information from the image is placed on top of it, so that you no longer see it. Let's start the exercise!

Open and crop the image

Before we can start retouching, we first open and then crop the image.

1. Tap *Import and Open* in the Photoshop Home screen and choose *Files* (**Figure 6.01**).

Figure 6.01 Place an image.

2. Open the exercise files and choose *old-photo* (**Figure 6.02**).

Figure 6.02 Select old-photo.

The image was scanned a little crooked, creating a white border along the outer edges, but we can remove that border by cropping the image.

3. Select the *Crop tool* in the toolbar (**Figure 6.03**).

You'll enter the *Crop and Rotate* workspace (**Figure 6.04**). You can crop by dragging the handles at the edge of the crop rectangle or rotate by dragging anywhere outside the image away from the handles, and the wheel below the image displays the current rotation angle.

Figure 6.03
Crop tool

Figure 6.04 Crop and rotate the image.

4. Rotate the photo about *0.7 degrees,* and then crop it until the white edges are gone. Tap *Done* when you're finished.

Remove the blemishes

Now we're ready to start retouching the photo. As you can see, there are quite a lot of spots and damage on it. We'll remove these using the Spot Healing Brush tool. This tool can retouch on the original layer directly, but I prefer not to do that because I like to work non-destructively. If you retouch on the original layer, you change it permanently, making it more difficult to undo steps later and return to the original image. Instead, we'll first create a new layer and configure the Spot Healing Brush to retouch on that new layer. The original layer then remains intact.

1. Create a new layer by tapping the *New Layer* button in the taskbar on the right side of the screen. Then choose *New Layer* (**Figure 6.05**).
2. Double-tap the layer name in the Layers panel and change the layer name to *Retouching* (**Figure 6.06**).
3. Now select the *Spot Healing Brush* tool (**Figure 6.07**).

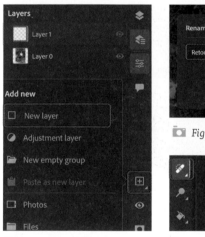

Figure 6.06 Rename Layer

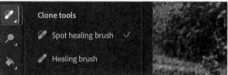

Figure 6.05 New Layer

Figure 6.07 Spot Healing Brush

4. When the Spot Healing Brush is selected, you'll see the *Tool Options* panel. You can enlarge your brush there, but you'll also see three dots at the bottom. Tap those to open the *Spot Healing Brush Settings* (**Figure 6.08**).
5. Enable *Sample All Layers*. This allows you to retouch on the top retouching layer, while Photoshop uses information—samples—from the layers below. If Sample All Layers was disabled, you'd be able to retouch on the original layer only.
6. Set the brush size to approximately *20 pixels* (**Figure 6.08**). Because *Use Pressure for Size* is enabled, you can also use stylus pressure to change the brush size.

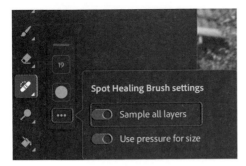

Spot Healing Brush settings

Sample all layers

Use pressure for size

Figure 6.08 Sample All Layers

7. Now pinch with two fingers to zoom in the photo and better see all the details.

8. Draw on the white spots and blemishes, step by step. You'll see a dark gray spot at first, but as soon as you release your stylus, Photoshop will replace the pixels of that spot with pixels from the surrounding area, seamlessly blending the replaced pixels with the existing ones. As a result, you won't see the spot anymore. If you make a mistake, tap two fingers to undo the step. Below you can see before (**Figure 6.09**) and after retouching (**Figure 6.10**).

9. Go through the entire photo until every speck is gone. I personally find this a calming process, but, I also know that it makes some people really nervous. I hope it makes you nice and calm too. If not, remember you can always undo.

Figure 6.09 Before

Figure 6.10 After

10. The retouched image looks like **Figure 6.11**. All the corrections were done in the Retouching layer. To take a look at the corrections, turn off the bottom layer by tapping the eye icon next to the layer name in the Layers panel. The result looks like **Figure 6.12**. Tap the eye icon again to turn the layer back on.

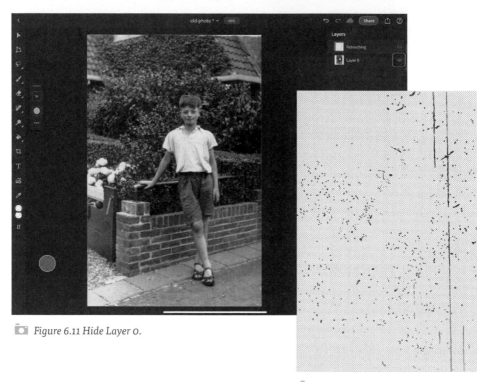

Figure 6.11 Hide Layer 0.

Figure 6.12 All corrections

11. Now tap the Retouching layer's eye icon to turn off the top layer so you can take a good look at the differences between the original and the retouched photo.

Improving light with Curves

The Spot Healing Brush took care of the main retouching, but we can perform a few extra actions to make the photo even nicer. First, we'll change the exposure to slightly reduce contrast in the midtones; then in the next sections we'll add a tint and vignette.

1. In the taskbar on the right side of the screen, tap the + icon and tap *Adjustment Layer* to add an adjustment layer (**Figure 6.13**).
2. Tap *Curves* (**Figure 6.14**). A Curves layer is added to the Layers panel now.

Note that we don't need to create a clipped adjustment layer this time. A clipped adjustment layer is linked and applied to only the layer (or layer group) directly below it. Because we want to adjust both the retouching layer and the old photo layer, we'll use a normal adjustment layer to apply the adjustments to all underlying layers.

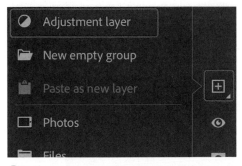

Figure 6.13 Add a new adjustment layer.

Figure 6.14 Curves

3. Now adjust the diagonal line in Curves to look like **Figure 6.15**. Add the nodes by tapping the diagonal line, and drag them up or down. For more information about Curves, see page 64.

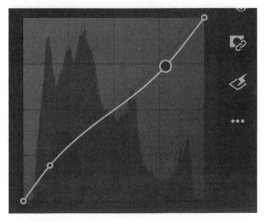

Figure 6.15 Adjust Curves.

As you can see, we lowered the contrast in the image with this Curves layer. The shadows (the little node on the left) have been pulled up, making the shadows lighter. The highlights (the node on the right) have been made darker by slightly pulling the node down.

Sepia effect with Hue/Saturation

After lowering the contrast, we'll add a sepia effect using a Hue/Saturation adjustment layer.

1. Select the Curves layer in the Layers panel so the adjustment layer you're about to add will be placed on top of it.
2. Tap the + icon in the taskbar and choose *Adjustment Layer* (**Figure 6.16**).
3. Tap *Hue/Saturation* (**Figure 6.17**) to specify the new adjustment layer's type.

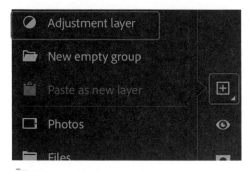

Figure 6.16 Add a new adjustment layer.

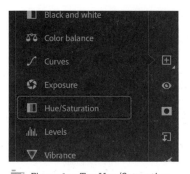

Figure 6.17 Tap Hue/Saturation.

We can directly adjust the settings in the *Layer Properties* panel now (**Figure 6.18**).

Figure 6.18 Adjust Hue/Saturation.

4. Tap the *Colorize* option at the bottom of the panel. This will turn all the underlying layers into the color tint you choose in *Hue*.

5. Set *Hue* to about 42 degrees (this is the color tone yellow/orange).

6. Set *Saturation* to about 9. This controls the saturation of the chosen color.

The photo now has a sepia effect. You can, of course, choose a different hue, adjust the saturation or turn off the sepia tint altogether if you don't like the addition.

Vignette with Curves and selections

This photo calls for a bit of a vignette: a slightly darker, soft, oval area around the photo. In Chapter 4, we added such a vignette in Lightroom, but you can easily create the same effect with a Curves adjustment layer and an elliptical selection Let's try it.

1. Select the *Marquee Ellipse* tool in the toolbar (**Figure 6.19**).

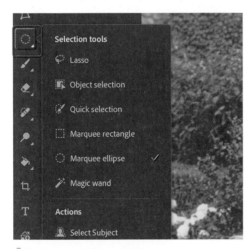

Figure 6.19 Marquee Ellipse

2. With this tool, draw an oval selection around the boy. Start dragging about one third from the top-left corner of the canvas, then drag all the way to the bottom right, as shown in **Figure 6.20**.

3. If we were to add a Curves layer at this point, we'd darken the area within the selection. We don't want to do that. So, tap *Invert* in the *Active Selection Properties bar* to invert the selection. Only the outside area is selected now (**Figure 6.21**).

Figure 6.20 *Draw an elliptical selection.* Figure 6.21 *Invert the selection.*

When we add and adjust a Curves adjustment layer, only the selected area is adjusted, because the selection is converted into a Curves layer mask: The selected area becomes white (reveals the Curves layer), everything else becomes black (conceals the Curves layer).

4. Tap the + icon in the taskbar. Next, choose *Adjustment Layer* and then *Curves* to add a Curves adjustment layer.
5. In the *Layer Properties* panel in the *Curves* section, darken the selection by dragging down the node (the little circle) in the upper-right corner (**Figure 6.22**).

The disadvantage now is that the edge is quite hard. That doesn't look good. Let's soften this edge in the next step.

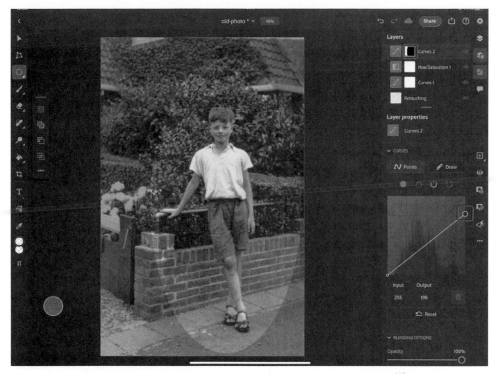

Figure 6.22 Darken the image with Curves.

Softening an edge can be done in several ways. This time we'll choose the *Gaussian Blur* effect on the Curves 2 layer mask, which allows us to blur the edges.

6. Make sure the *Curves 2 layer mask* is selected in the Layers panel (**Figure 6.22**).
7. In the taskbar on the right side of the screen, tap the *Filters and Adjustments* button and choose *Gaussian Blur* (**Figure 6.23**).

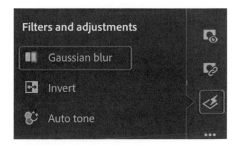

Figure 6.23 Gaussian Blur

8. You now enter the *Gaussian Blur* workspace. It varies from case to case how much blur is needed to get the best effect. In this case, try *150 pixels* (**Figure 6.24**). This creates a nice soft edge. The vignette is now very subtle, but does provide a focus on the subject.

Figure 6.24 Adjust Gaussian Blur.

9. Tap *Done*.
10. If you find the vignette too light, or too dark, you can still adjust the settings in the *Properties panel*. Drag the node on the right down to make the vignette darker. Drag it up to make it lighter (**Figure 6.25**).
11. That's it! You can now tap the *Export button* to save the photo as a JPG, or return to the *Home screen* by tapping the little arrow at the top left of the screen.

Figure 6.25 Adjust Curves.

Figure 6.26 The end result

The Clone Stamp tool

In the previous exercise, we used the Spot Healing Brush, the smartest of all retouching tools. Because it figures out for itself what it will "draw back" on a spot or other element, it requires almost no work on your part. That same "hands-off" approach, however, means that sometimes the elements the Spot Healing Brush chooses to redraw yield undesirable results.

In those cases, the Clone Stamp tool can be a good alternative.

I do have to confess that I don't use the Clone Stamp tool very often on the iPad. That's because the Spot Healing Brush works so well. But, sometimes you need to be able to control exactly which element you put where. To demonstrate, we'll remove an unsightly light fixture from a brick wall using the Clone Stamp tool in the following short exercise.

1. Open the file *clone-stamp* from the exercise folder. To do so, in the Photoshop Home screen, go to the *Import and Open* button, choose *Files* and look for the file (**Figure 6.27**).

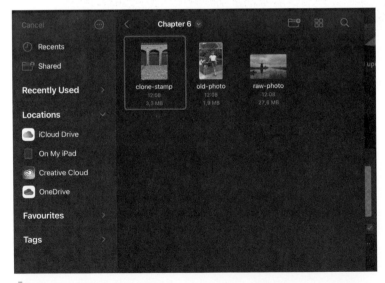

📷 *Figure 6.27 Open clone-stamp.*

2. As in the previous retouching exercise, we'll first create a new layer so we can work non-destructively. To do so, tap the + icon in the toolbar on the right side of the screen and choose *New Layer*.

3. A new layer is created in the Layers panel. Double-tap the layer name and change the name to *Clone* (**Figure 6.28**).

4. Select the *Clone Stamp* tool in the toolbar (**Figure 6.29**).

5. We'll draw on the new layer in the next steps, and sample pieces from the underlying layer. To do that, we need to change some settings in the tool options to ensure the Clone Stamp tool is allowed to sample on the current layer and the layer below. Therefore, tap the three dots at the bottom of the *Tool Options* panel, and choose *Current and Below* in the *Sample* section (**Figure 6.30**).

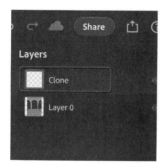
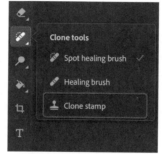

Figure 6.28 Rename the layer.   Figure 6.29 Clone Stamp tool   Figure 6.30 Current and Below

6. Set the brush size to about *40 pixels*. You can set that size, as with the regular brushes and the Spot Healing Brush, at the top of the *Tool Options panel*.

We'll remove the lamp in this image. That means we have to draw a piece of the brick wall over the lamp. To do that, we need to choose a source for the Clone Stamp tool to use. In our case, that's the joint at the bottom left of a dark brown brick. The next step is to draw that source over the subject you want to remove (the lamp). The important thing is to choose a source that fits nicely with the part you're going to paint away.

7. To choose the clone source, press and hold your finger in the center of the touch shortcut (**Figure 6.31**). While doing this, tap with your stylus once, exactly on the bottom-left corner of one of the dark brown stones. This will temporarily store that part of the image in the Clone Stamp tool, until you set a new clone source.

Figure 6.31 *Use the touch shortcut to set the clone source.*

8. Now that the clone source is set, you can start drawing. But, be careful. It's important to place your stylus on the bottom-left side of a similar stone, one or two stones to the left of the clone source. Otherwise, the joints and other stones will not connect properly (**Figure 6.32**). You now copy one brick exactly on top of the other brick.

Figure 6.32 *Start cloning with the Clone Stamp tool.*

As you draw, you see the crosshairs of the clone source moving back and forth, as if it were still attached to your brush. Your brush is currently drawing exactly what's at the position of the crosshairs. You actually copy the clone source area to the lamp and the area around it.

9. Release your stylus occasionally to commit the cloning action, and then continue drawing. The result you're aiming for looks like **Figure 6.33**.

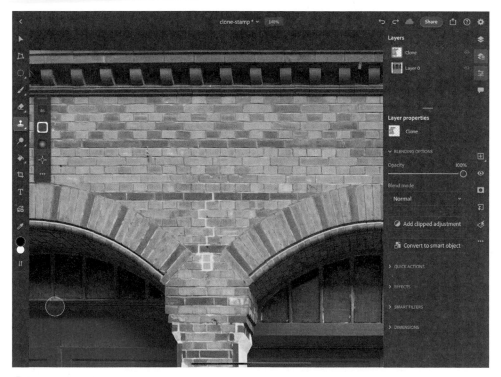

Figure 6.33 *The end result.*

Sometimes you'll need to set up a new clone source by pressing the touch shortcut again and then tapping a new area. In my case, this wasn't necessary, so I could just keep on drawing. While drawing, be sure to release your stylus from the iPad occasionally. Only then does cloning become final. If you don't do this, there is a chance that you'll redraw a removed part again in a different place.

10. In the Layer panel, turn off the bottom layer with the eye icon (in my case that layer is called *Layer 0*). This way you can clearly see what you've drawn on the *Clone* layer (**Figure 6.34**). As you can see, cloning is nothing more than copying a piece from one place to another, to ensure you no longer see the original objects.

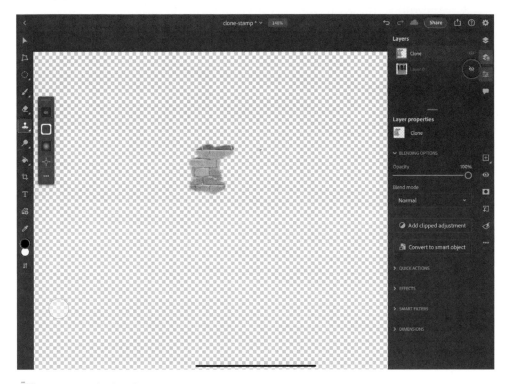

Figure 6.34 *The clone layer.*

11. Now turn the bottom layer back on by tapping the eye icon again.

That was our short, but nice, clone stamping exercise! In the next exercise, we'll continue retouch a raw image after doing some preliminary editing in Lightroom for mobile.

Raw photo editing

In Photoshop on the iPad, you can perform basic operations on raw files. You'll see an example of that at the end of this chapter. But, my preference is to edit raw photos in a much more comprehensive editing program: Lightroom for mobile. Lightroom works seamlessly with Photoshop. When you're done editing your image in Lightroom, you can send it to Photoshop, where you can continue working on it.

The process of editing a raw photo on an iPad is therefore much like the workflow many photographers have on the desktop: editing and organizing photos in Lightroom and then continuing to edit in Photoshop.

What is a raw file?

A raw file is simply the "raw," unprocessed information stored from the camera sensor on the memory card in your camera. A raw file is a bit like the negative in analog photography that you used to have to develop first.

Most photographers choose to shoot in raw format, because they can do much more with the file afterwards than with a JPG file, which contains considerably less information. On the other hand, a JPG has a much smaller file size too, so your memory card will not fill up as quickly as with raw files.

Most camera brands have their own raw format. For example, Nikon uses NEF, Canon uses CR2 and CRW, and Sony uses ARW. In the following exercise, we'll edit a NEF file.

The editing process

In Chapter 4, we sent our photo composition from Photoshop to Lightroom so that we could do the final post-processing there. That's an incredibly useful method, but usually this operation will go the other way around when you're working with raw files. In that case, you first load a raw file into Lightroom and then send it to Photoshop for post-processing, like retouching or combining the photo into a composition. In the upcoming exercise, we'll go through that process. First we'll "develop" the raw file in Lightroom, then send it to Photoshop where we'll retouch the photo. Of course, this is a book about Photoshop on the iPad, so I'm not covering all of Lightroom's capabilities. But you'll learn some commonly used features that will quickly get you started.

Editing raw photos in Lightroom

Let's load a raw file in Lightroom first.

1. Open Lightroom. Make sure the app is installed.
2. In Lightroom, tap the *Add Photos* button at the bottom (**Figure 6.35**). In this case, choose *From Files* because, as in Photoshop, we are loading files from our iPad Files app.

Figure 6.35 Add photos from files.

3. Navigate to this chapter's exercise folder and tap *raw-photo* (**Figure 6.36**). The photo will be loaded into the current Lightroom library or the current Lightroom album. If the photo disappears among all your other photos, tap the *Recently Added* view; the raw-photo file should be at the top.

Figure 6.36 Choose the photo.

4. Tap the thumbnail in the library to open the photo (**Figure 6.37**).

Figure 6.37 Tap the photo in your library.

The photo will be loaded. The screen you enter now is the same as when we sent our photo composition to Lightroom in Chapter 4 (**Figure 6.38**). On the right side are all the tabs with editing options, and on the far right you'll find a number of other tools. We'll use a few of them later. The photo is quite dark now and does need some adjustments. I'll walk you through the editing process step by step. Feel free to experiment yourself. You can't really do anything wrong.

Figure 6.38 Lightroom Edit workspace

5. For raw files, I always start with the *Optics* panel (**Figure 6.39**). This lets you enable the standard lens corrections. This photo is shot with a wide-angle lens that has mild vignetting along the edges. Furthermore, the photo is slightly more bulgy than it should be. Therefore, turn on *Enable Lens Corrections*. You'll immediately see that the photo becomes less dark along the edges and less bulgy. This is also a good starting point when changing the exposure of the photo.

6. Tapping the AI-powered *Auto* button is often a great first step. But since we're starting from scratch in this exercise, continue at the top with the *Light* panel. I chose the following settings (**Figure 6.40**):
Exposure: +1,00 (lightens the picture slightly)
Contrast: +10 (increases contrast)
Highlights: –5 (highlights slightly darker)
Shadows: +89 (shadows much lighter)
Whites: +13 (whites slightly lighter)
Blacks: –10 (blacks slightly darker)

7. Then open the *Color* panel (**Figure 6.41**).
8. Here you can adjust white balance and brightness of colors, among other things. These are my settings:

   Temperature: 5528K (makes color temperature slightly colder)

   Tint: +20 (brings a little more magenta to the scene)

   Vibrance: +9 (boosts less saturated colors).

Figure 6.39 Optics

Figure 6.40 Light

Figure 6.41 Color

9. In the *Effects* panel, set the *Texture* slider to +20. This adds contrast around patterns with details such as wood or grass, although not at the finer level of detail that Sharpening enhances (**Figure 6.42**).
10. Finally, adjust the *Detail* panel. You can sharpen the image with the *Sharpening* slider there. I set the sharpening amount to 50 (**Figure 6.43**).

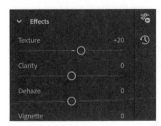

Figure 6.42 Effects

Figure 6.43 Detail

Selective edits

The edits we just applied are performed on the entire photo. Lightroom also has the ability to apply edits to a selective area using masks. I regularly use the *Select Sky* feature, which uses artificial intelligence to select the sky really quickly. This can be useful when you want to accentuate a cloudy sky, for example. The following exercise shows you how to do this.

1. On the right side of the screen, select the *Masking* tool ⬚ (**Figure 6.44**).
2. You're now in the *Masking* workspace. Tap the + at the bottom right of the screen. The *Create New Mask* menu now shows a variety of ways to create a mask or selection. Choose *Select Sky* to automatically select the sky (**Figure 6.45**).

Figure 6.44 Masking workspace

Figure 6.45 Create New Mask menu

You now see a red overlay on top of the sky (**Figure 6.46**). That means that a mask has been created for the sky. The mask menu at the bottom right of the screen shows a mask thumbnail that's black and white like the layer mask icon you saw in Photoshop. On the

Figure 6.46 The red overlay represents the new sky mask..

bottom left side of the screen are two buttons that can invert and delete the mask. In the panels on the right, you can adjust the settings. These are then applied only to the selected sky.

3. In the *Light* tab, set *Exposure* to –0.30, *Highlights* to –100, *Shadows* to –100 and *Blacks* to –50 (**Figure 6.47**). This makes the sky more present and dramatic (**Figure 6.48**).

4. Tap *Done* at the bottom right when you're finished. After you tap Done, the panels edit the entire image again, not just the masked area.

Figure 6.48 The edited sky.

Figure 6.47 Light

5. Finally, let's crop the photo. I like the proportion of the photo just a little better when the horizon is positioned about a third from the bottom of the photo. You can do this with the *Crop & Rotate* tool 🔁 on the right side of the screen. I dragged the bottom crop handle up a bit, as you can see in **Figure 6.49**. Once you drag, you'll see two horizontal lines. I placed the lower one on the horizon If the aspect ratio padlock icon is locked, tap to unlock it so that you can crop the bottom without affecting the other sides.

6. Tap *Done* at the bottom right when you're finished.

Figure 6.49 Crop the image.

Editing and retouching in Photoshop

Now that we're finished with the global editing, let's go to Photoshop so we can continue editing the photo there.

1. At the top right of the Lightroom screen, you'll find a *Share* button. Tap this button (**Figure 6.50**). The Share menu appears, where you'll see many of the familiar share options.

2. Tap *Edit in Photoshop* (**Figure 6.50**).

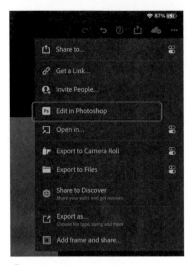

 Figure 6.50 Edit in Photoshop

Photoshop opens. A connection has now been established between Lightroom and Photoshop. You can edit the image in Photoshop and send it back to Lightroom after that, using the *Send to Lightroom* button (**Figure 6.51**). But, we won't do that just yet, because we're going to remove some power pylons and other unwanted elements first.

 Figure 6.51 The image in Photoshop

3. As in the previous exercises, we'll first create a new layer. Tap the + icon in the taskbar on the right side of the screen. Then tap *New Layer*. A new layer appears in the Layers panel (**Figure 6.52**). If you like, you can rename the layer. I didn't do that in the example since we're only working on this one layer.

4. In the toolbar, select the *Spot Healing Brush* (it's probably hidden behind the Clone Stamp tool). Then tap the three dots at the bottom of the tool options for more options. Make sure *Sample All Layers* is enabled so you can retouch on the new layer we just created (**Figure 6.53**).

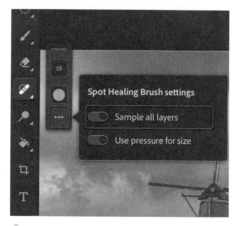

 *Figure 6.52 New layer*   *Figure 6.53 Sample All Layers*

5. Set the brush size to about 30 to 40 pixels.

Now we can start retouching. We'll mainly remove the power pylons. They do look a bit out of place in this beautiful Dutch Unesco heritage landscape known as Kinderdijk.

6. Zoom in your photo, and draw over the power lines and the power pylons. Drawing piece by piece and not all at once will generally make the result more beautiful. Make a mistake, or really not satisfied with the result? Tap with two fingers to undo the last step (**Figure 6.54**).

7. Go through the whole image like this. For example, I also removed some of the prominent apartments on the right side of the photo.

📷 *Figure 6.54 Use the Spot Healing Brush.*

Content Aware Fill

If you want to remove larger, harder-to-remove parts from an image, you can use *Content Aware Fill*. With this function, you can, just like in Photoshop on the desktop, let Photoshop automatically fill everything within a selection with parts from the surrounding area, resulting in the removal of everything within that selection. This will save you a lot of time! In the next steps, we'll select and delete the part that sticks out on the left side of the photo.

1. First, select the bottom layer in the Layers panel (**Figure 6.55**), because Content Aware Fill samples on the selected layer only.
2. Select the *Lasso* tool in the toolbar and draw a lasso around the part on the left side of the picture, as shown in **Figure 6.55**.
3. Now tap *Content Aware Fill* in the *Active Selection Properties* bar at the bottom of the screen (**Figure 6.56**). Magical! The contents of the selection are now intelligently filled with elements from the surrounding area. If the results are not as expected, you can always undo and try it again.

Figure 6.55 Make a Lasso selection.

Figure 6.56 Tap Content Aware Fill.

4. Tap *Deselect* in the *Active Selection Properties* bar to deselect the selection.

5. If necessary, you can clean up unwanted elements with the Spot Healing Brush tool. In **Figure 6.56**, for example, you can see a number of randomly placed dashes and a piece of a high-voltage pylon. It's just a little work to get rid of those elements by drawing over them with the Spot Healing Brush.

6. Finally, all distracting elements have been removed. You can now do two things: Send the photo back to Lightroom via the *Send to Lightroom* button, or tap the three dots next to that button. If you tap the three dots, the *Create Photoshop Cloud Document* button appears. Tapping that button creates a new Photoshop Cloud Document that can also be opened in the desktop version of Photoshop. Tap *Create Photoshop Cloud Document* (**Figure 6.57**), but feel free to test out how the Send to Lightroom feature works. You can then continue editing your image directly in Lightroom.

Figure 6.57 Create Photoshop Cloud Document

The end result

Of course, you can edit this photo in an incredibly wide variety of ways. By playing with all the different options in Lightroom and Photoshop, you'll probably end up getting the result you had in mind.

Finally, I used the Export button in Photoshop to export the photo as a JPG via Publish and Export. You can see the result below (**Figure 6.58**).

You've probably noticed that Lightroom and Photoshop on the iPad are a very powerful and indispensable combination. Together, these apps make your iPad a complete photo-editing workstation that allows you to perform the most commonly used photo operations on the go and in your studio.

Figure 6.58 The final result

Extra: Image size

In Photoshop on the iPad, you can also resize your entire Photoshop document. Is your image too large, or just too small? You can change the pixel dimensions by adding or removing pixels. Note that enlarging an image is not without risk. Photoshop is very good at adding pixels, but especially smaller images will not improve in quality.

I usually resize an image on a copy of the original Photoshop document, because otherwise the original Cloud Document will be adjusted. So, first duplicate the Cloud Document, or export the image as a JPG, PNG, TIFF or PSD. Open that image in Photoshop, and then resize it. Here's how to adjust the image size and resolution.

GEAR ICON: When you tap the gear icon at the top right of the Edit workspace, the *Document Properties* panel opens. Tap *Image Size* to change the image size (**Figure 6.59**).

Figure 6.59 Document Properties

RESAMPLE: In the *Image size* window (**Figure 6.60**), you'll first see the *Resample* option, which is enabled by default. Resample changes the number of pixels in the image, which may be useful if the image will be scaled up or down by a large amount, or if the pixel dimensions must change. Without Resample, the image keeps the exact amount of pixels while only the resolution is changed.

IMAGE SIZE: If you want to change the number of pixels, always make sure *Resample* is enabled. You can then change *Units* to *Pixels* and change the size in the *W* (width) and *H* (height) fields. Make sure the lock icon is visible next to W and H so that your image is scaled proportionally.

RESOLUTION: Sometimes it's necessary to change the resolution—the number of pixels per inch—in the *Resolution* field, especially if you're going to submit your document for printing. A typical print resolution is 300 pixels per inch (ppi). Before changing the resolution, it's best to disable Resample to ensure that no pixels are added or removed. After that, you can safely change the resolution. As you change physical dimensions, such as Inches, the Resolution field updates to show you the ppi value at the physical dimensions you enter. If the ppi value is too low or too high for the physical dimensions, enable Resample and enter the ppi value you require. If the image is too small, you can enable *Resample* again, and increase the size of the image. Photoshop will then automatically add pixels. If Resample is enabled and the results aren't as expected, try a different option from the *Mode* menu, which changes how the resulting pixels are calculated.

Figure 6.60 Image Size

Extra: Edit raw images in Photoshop

In this chapter, we edited a raw image in Lightroom and then sent it to Photoshop. This is still my favorite method, because Lightroom offers a lot of advanced editing features. However, if you want to apply just a few basic adjustments to a raw image, you can also open it directly with Photoshop on the iPad. This process should be familiar if you have used the Camera Raw plug-in for Photoshop on the desktop. This is how to do it:

1. Open Photoshop on the iPad, go to *Import and Open* and choose *Files*.
2. Go to the exercise folder and choose *raw-photo*.

Because you're opening a NEF file (a raw image), Photoshop opens the raw-editing workspace first (**Figure 6.61**). This workspace is very similar to Lightroom, but has fewer features. For example, it's missing the advanced masking capabilities.

3. You can open the *Light*, *Color*, *Effects*, *Detail* and *Optics* tabs to change the settings, just as we did in Lightroom.

Figure 6.61 Edit a raw photo in Photoshop.

4. When you're finished, tap the *Import As* button in the upper-right corner of the window (**Figure 6.62**).

5. Choose *Import as Smart Object*. The photo will open in the Photoshop Edit workspace.

Figure 6.62 Import as Smart Object

The advantage of editing a raw image in Photoshop, is that you can import your edited photo as a *Smart Object*. This keeps the raw edits stored in this Smart Object layer, which allows you to adjust those raw edits later, even after closing the document. A Smart Object has many other advantages, but because Photoshop on the iPad has limited capabilities at this time, I won't go into them now.

You can see that the layer's thumbnail looks slightly different. This indicates the layer is a Smart Object (**Figure 6.63**).

6. Now double-tap this layer thumbnail. You'll now return to the raw-editing workspace. Here you can adjust all the settings again.

TIP: If you open this document via Cloud Documents in Photoshop on the desktop, you can double click the layer thumbnail to open it in Camera Raw for the desktop, which offers a wider range of features than Camera Raw for iPad..

📷 *Figure 6.63 Double-tap the layer thumbnail.*

Chapter 7

Frankie Cihi

MURALS IN PHOTOSHOP

Born and raised in Tokyo, Japan, Frankie Cihi's work ranges from digital illustrations to large-scale murals that can be seen in public spaces around the world. Fascinated by color, the natural world, as well as her multicultural heritage, she often blends traditional Japanese textile patterns together with organic motifs in her work. A firm believer in creative collaborations, Frankie regularly produces artwork with such brands as Adobe, Google, Starbucks and Instagram, and continues to work across various industries.

Name:	Frankie Cihi
Residence:	Tokyo, Japan
Finds inspiration:	All around her and in her multicultural roots
Favorite tool:	Brushes
Most used tools:	Brushes and selections
Other favorites:	Adobe Fresco
Best advice:	Just go try it, look it up on Google, working on the iPad is so easy!

How do you work with Photoshop on the iPad?

I create large wall paintings, also called murals. I usually first take a photo of the building on which the mural will be painted. After that, I load that photo into Photoshop on the iPad and paint the mural on top of it. That first concept allows the client to immediately see what the end result will look like. At the same time, drawing on an iPad makes it much easier for me to estimate in advance what I'm going to draw on the building. There's much more room for experimentation because I can try things out without making big mistakes. In the end, that still produces the best results. I use Photoshop on the iPad primarily for painting and drawing. The program has a wonderfully simple workspace that gives me a nice result quickly. I also like the fact that the iPad is so compact and mobile. I can take it anywhere, and sometimes I find myself drawing in the park or at an espresso bar.

Besides murals, do you sometimes create other things in Photoshop on the iPad?

Yes definitely! The funny thing is that while drawing murals, I found out that my concepts in Photoshop on the iPad already looked like beautiful, ready-made artworks. That's why I now create digital illustrations more often for big brands and companies. For example, I recently designed the packaging for Porsche Japan's sustainable water bottle campaign, and I created a design for Clinique that was printed on their gift wrapping cloth for the holidays. Another project I really enjoyed was designing the fabric lining for a suitcase brand called AWW here in Japan.

What iPad are you currently working on?

The iPad Pro 11-inch and the Apple Pencil 2. I don't have the largest iPad because it's very important to me that I can easily carry it with me.

Do you combine Photoshop on the iPad with other apps?

Yes, I'm a big fan of *Adobe Fresco*. Fresco is a more extensive drawing app with all kinds of *pixel and vector brushes* that I really like to use. For example, I sketch initial concepts for car stickers on top of a photo of a car with Fresco's vector brushes, because car stickers eventually have to be delivered to the printer as a vector. I then load that sketch into *Adobe Illustrator* on the desktop and refine the vector drawing there. This method seems a bit complicated, but I don't draw in Illustrator on the desktop as intuitively as I do on an iPad. It works best for me if I start on the iPad and then continue working on the desktop.

By the way, painting with Fresco doesn't mean that I no longer paint in Photoshop on the iPad. In fact, Photoshop has the advantage of having more extensive capabilities with layers and pixel images. That's why I like the combination of all the apps together.

Are there any tools you miss in Photoshop on the iPad?

Yes, on my iPhone, for example, I have apps like Photoshop Fix installed. Photoshop Fix has all kinds of handy one-click fixes, like smoothing skin. I'd love to see Photoshop on the iPad get more of those handy quick actions. It'd also be helpful if Photoshop on the iPad had more variety in the default brushes, even though I know you can import brushes. But overall, I'm already really satisfied with how Photoshop works on an iPad. If I really miss features, I quickly open my iPad file via Cloud Documents in Photoshop on the desktop.

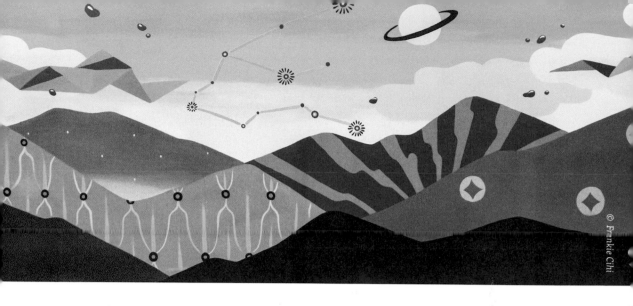

Do you have any tips for new users?

When it comes to iPad apps, I think you should just go ahead and try. The apps are very easy to use, and by trying them yourself you'll develop your own way of working. If you run into problems or can't find something, you can always look it up on Google. So just go do it!

Chapter 8

Social media

DESIGN YOUR OWN BANNER FOR SOCIAL MEDIA

Photoshop is a perfect program for designing your own graphics for social media. In this chapter, you'll create an Instagram banner. You'll see how easy it is to install fonts on your iPad, how to send your Photoshop document to Adobe Fresco and paint with watercolor brushes, how to select hair and much more.

Create a banner for social media

In this exercise, we'll design a banner for social media using a variety of fun techniques. Because we've already talked about some of the techniques in previous exercises, I'll describe those more briefly here. You'll learn plenty new too, such as how to add fonts to the iPad and paint in Adobe Fresco. Have fun!

The finish and start

Figure 8.01 shows our final result: an image you could use as an Instagram Story. To get there, we first need to create a new document.

📷 *Figure 8.01 The end result*

1. In the Photoshop Home screen, tap *Create New*.
2. Go to the *Social* tab, choose *Instagram Story*, and tap the Create button. Photoshop creates a new document at the default size of an Instagram Story, 1080 pixels by 1920 pixels (**Figure 8.02**).

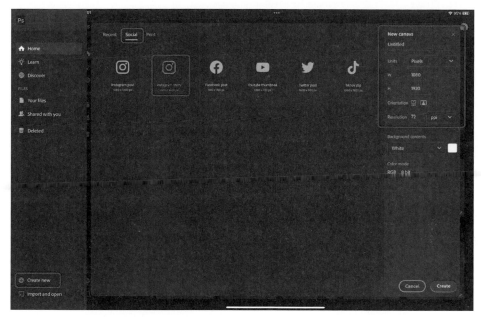

📷 *Figure 8.02 Create a new document.*

3. Now place the image of the giraffe: Tap the *Place Photo* button in the toolbar and choose *Files*.

4. Navigate to the exercise files and choose *giraffe* (**Figure 8.03**).

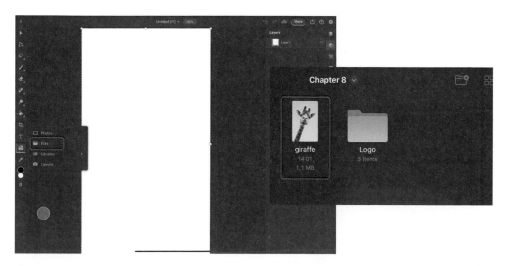

📷 *Figure 8.03 Place the giraffe.*

5. Enlarge the giraffe a bit and place it in roughly the same position as in **Figure 8.04**. Tap *Done*.

Figure 8.04 Scale the giraffe.

Selecting and masking

Now we need to remove the giraffe's background. Although there is a Remove Background button, we'll use Select Subject and Refine Edge first to make sure the fine hairs are selected properly. After that, we'll create a layer mask.

1. Tap and hold the selection tools in the toolbar for a moment, or double-tap them. Because the giraffe is an easily distinguishable subject in the photo, you can choose *Select Subject* (**Figure 8.05**) to select it automatically.

Figure 8.05 Select Subject

2. The selection is almost perfect. The giraffe's hair could be selected a little better. To fix this, tap *Refine Edge* in the *Active Selection Properties* bar at the bottom of the screen (**Figure 8.06**).

Figure 8.06 *Tap Refine Edge.*

3. You're now in the *Refine Edge* workspace. Make sure the *Overlay* mode is selected under *View Mode* in the Properties panel (**Figure 8.07**). In Overlay mode, the area outside the selection turns red, making it easier to see the selection edge that you are refining.

Figure 8.07 *Set View Mode to Overlay.*

4. Set the brush in the brush options on the left side of the screen to about *30 pixels* (**Figure 8.08**).

With the *Refine Edge* brush you can draw along hairs that have not been properly selected yet. For example, some hairs still have a light background, while others are not selected at all. (You can also use this brush when you select people and want to select their hairs properly.)

5. The *Refine Edge* brush is automatically selected in the Refine Edge workspace. So you don't need to select a brush and can draw directly along the edges of the giraffe's hairs. Zoom in so you can clearly see what's happening, and draw carefully over the hairs to add them to the selection. With the Refine Edge brush only draw over the edges of the subject and never on the inside, as this can cause some inner areas to become transparent. In **Figure 8.08** you can see that the hairs are not yet nicely selected; in **Figure 8.09** they are.

Figure 8.08 Before   *Figure 8.09 After*

6. Also be sure to draw along the hairs on the eyelashes and on other hairy areas around the giraffe.

7. Tap *Done* when you're finished. The selection looks perfect!

8. You probably already have an idea of what we're going to do next. The giraffe is selected, and we want to hide the background, so we'll create a mask: Tap the *Mask* button in the Active Selection Properties bar at the bottom of the screen (**Figure 8.10**). By the way, you can also tap the identical mask button in the taskbar on the right side of the screen.

Figure 8.10 Create a layer mask.

Photoshop now adds the mask to the layer in the Layers panel and hides the background of the giraffe (**Figure 8.11**).

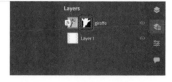

Figure 8.11 Layer mask in the Layers panel

Add your logo to Creative Cloud Libraries

You could now place the Wild Park logo by tapping the Place Photo button and choosing Files. But, suppose you need this logo often. Wouldn't it be convenient if you always find the logo in one place *and* in all your favorite Creative Cloud programs? You can, if you use *Creative Cloud Libraries*.

You can create a Creative Cloud Library in almost any Adobe program by going to the Libraries panel. Think of a library like a container, where you collect and store all your design elements—like logos and brand colors—for a company or project. You can get those design elements right out of that library when you need them.

Photoshop on the iPad can place elements from libraries into your document, but unfortunately cannot yet create a library or put design elements into it. But, there is a solution; in fact, you can use the Creative Cloud iPad app for this. In the following steps, you'll see how to create a library, put a logo in it and place the logo in Photoshop on the iPad.

1. Open the *Creative Cloud* app.
2. Go to the *Files* section and tap the *Libraries* tab (**Figure 8.12**).

If you have created libraries before, you'll see them here. If you haven't, you'll only see the default *My Library*.

3. Now tap the *New Library* button 🗂 to create a new library. (**Figure 8.12**).

Figure 8.12 *Create a new library in the Creative Cloud app.*

4. Name the library *Wild Park assets* in the New Library dialog box and tap *Create* (**Figure 8.13**).

📷 *Figure 8.13 Rename the library.*

5. Tap the *Wild Park assets* library to open it (**Figure 8.14**). You might need to scroll down if you have already created more libraries.

📷 *Figure 8.14 Open the library.*

6. Now tap the + icon and choose *Upload Files* to upload a logo from the exercise files folder to the library (**Figure 8.15**).

7. In this chapter's exercise files folder, navigate to the *Logo* folder, then tap the *SVG* folder and choose *wild-park-logo* (**Figure 8.16**). Tap *Open* to upload the file to your library.

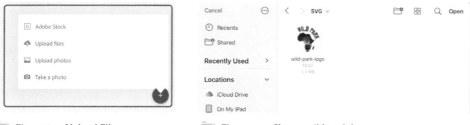

📷 *Figure 8.15 Upload Files* 📷 *Figure 8.16 Choose wild-park-logo.*

Your logo is now saved in the Wild Park assets library, and you can use it in any Creative Cloud app from now on.

By the way, I deliberately chose to upload an SVG (*Scalable Vector Graphics*) file. An SVG is a vector file, created in software like Adobe Illustrator. Because it's a vector file, your logo will remain sharp in all cases, as vector files are infinitely scalable.

Currently, though, Photoshop on the iPad flattens these vector files, turning them into PNG images. But, in all other Adobe apps, you do have the benefits of the SVG file.

Another note: In all other Adobe apps, placed assets are linked to the original file in the library by default. If you update the original file in the library, all placed files also change. This can be very useful if you change the color of frequently used design elements, for example. Unfortunately, Photoshop on the iPad doesn't currently support linked files either.

Place the logo in Photoshop

You can now place the logo from our library into Photoshop.

1. Launch Photoshop and make sure you have your social media banner open.
2. Tap the *Place Photo* button, choose *Libraries* (**Figure 8.17**) and then open the *Wild Park assets* library (**Figure 8.18**).
3. If you see a *Not Grouped* folder, tap it first, and then choose *wild-park-logo.svg* (**Figure 8.19**).

Figure 8.17 Place Photo

Figure 8.18 Wild Park assets

Figure 8.19 Wild-park-logo.svg

4. Position and scale the logo as shown in **Figure 8.20**.
5. Tap *Done* when you're finished.

Before we move on to the next exercise, I want to show you two other ways to place images in Photoshop.

Figure 8.20 Position and scale the logo.

Place an image using the camera

Another option you can use to place a photo is through the camera on your iPad. If you tap the Place Photo button and then Camera, the camera is activated. When you take a picture, the photo will then only be placed in Photoshop. This means it isn't added to Lightroom or Apple Photos, so your photo only exists in Photoshop. Frankie Cihi uses this option before she creates her murals. (You read about this in Chapter 7.)

Place an image using the Photos app

If you already have photos in the native iPad Photos app, you can also place them using the Place Photo button in the toolbar. When you tap Photos, Photoshop will bring you directly to the Photos app. You can then select a photo and place it in your document (**Figure 8.21**).

Figure 8.21 *Place from Photos*

Adding fonts to your iPad

In a moment we're going to add text to the social media banner, and we'll use a font that isn't yet on the iPad. The fun thing about a Creative Cloud subscription is that you have access to thousands of premium fonts through Adobe Fonts. You can download and activate those fonts to your iPad from Photoshop, as well as from the Creative Cloud app. The advantage of downloading and activating fonts through the Creative Cloud app is that those fonts will be available in other apps also. Fonts activated from Photoshop can be used in Photoshop only.

1. Open the *Creative Cloud* app on your iPad.
2. Go the *Fonts* section on the left side of the home screen (**Figure 8.22**) and tap the magnifying glass icon at the top right to search for a font.
3. Type *Chinese Rocks* in the search field, and tap Search on the virtual keyboard or Enter (Return for macOS) on a hardware keyboard.
4. Tap the font name to view the font family (**Figure 8.23**).
5. Tap the +-icon ⊕ next to the font to add the font to your iPad (**Figure 8.24**).
6. When the iPad asks if you want to install the font, choose *Install* (**Figure 8.25**). The font is now installed and can be used in all apps.

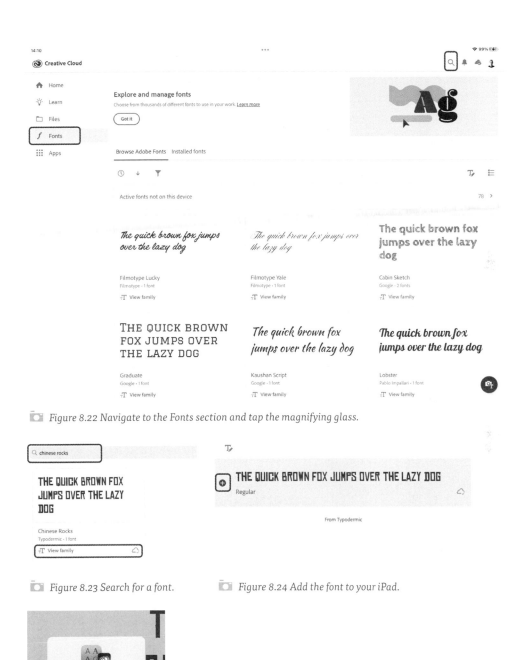

Figure 8.22 Navigate to the Fonts section and tap the magnifying glass.

Figure 8.23 Search for a font.

Figure 8.24 Add the font to your iPad.

Figure 8.25 Tap Install.

As you may have seen in **Figure 8.22**, there are a lot of fonts to choose from the Fonts section. It's worth taking a look and adding more fonts, because the default font set on an iPad is pretty limited. By the way, if you receive a document from someone else that contains an Adobe Font, that font will automatically be activated when you open the document in Photoshop. This applies to both the desktop and iPad versions of Photoshop.

Adding text

Now that we've added the Chinese Rocks font, we can use this font in Photoshop.

1. Go to Photoshop on the iPad and open the social media banner.
2. Tap the *Type* tool in the toolbar (**Figure 8.25**).

Figure 8.25 *The Type tool*

3. Tap somewhere above the giraffe on the place where you'd like to add text. You will now enter the Type workspace where you'll find all the text options on the right side of the screen. The Lorum Ipsum text that appears is just placeholder text, which disappears when you start typing.
4. On the right side of the screen, select the *Chinese Rocks* font in the *Fonts* section (**Figure 8.26**).
5. Type *Fantastic*, press Return and type *Wildlife!* (**Figure 8.27**).

Figure 8.26 Choose your font.

6. Now select the text by tapping and dragging your finger or stylus over it.
7. Now go back to Layer Properties by tapping the arrow ◀ next to Fonts (**Figure 8.26**).
8. In the *Layer Properties panel*, scroll down until you see the *Paragraph* options. Here you can set your paragraph options, like the alignment of your text. Tap the *Align Center button* to align the text in the center of the text frame (**Figure 8.27**).

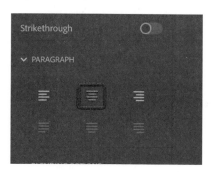

Figure 8.27 Center align your text.

9. Scroll back up in the Layer Properties panel and make the text larger at *Font Size*. Enlarge your text to *190 pixels* (**Figure 8.28**).

10. The distance between the lines is still fairly large. Therefore, move *Leading* towards about *170 pixels* (**Figure 8.28**).

11. Is your text not positioned correctly yet? Then you can move it with the ⊕ icon at the bottom of the text. Unlike in the desktop version of Photoshop, Smart Guides aren't available to help you see if the text is centered on the page. Hopefully that feature will be added to the iPad version in the not too distant future. For now, position the text by sight.

Figure 8.28 Change Font Size and Leading.

By the way, feel free to experiment with the other text options. The number of options is manageable, and you'll recognize most of the options from other software.

12. Tap *Done* when you're finished.

13. It would be nice to rotate the text a bit. To do this, activate the *Transform* tool ⬔ in the toolbar, or drag one of the transformation handles with the *Move* tool.

14. Drag the circle at the top of the text frame to rotate the text, or drag just outside the bounding box or handles (**Figure 8.29**).

15. Tap *Done* when you're finished.

Figure 8.29 Rotate the text.

In the next step, we'll open the Photoshop document in Adobe Fresco and start painting in the document there. Before we do that, we need to make sure that the latest version of the document is synced to the cloud. And, we also have to rename our document.

16. Tap the document name at the top of your screen (**Figure 8.30**).
17. Tap the document name in the popup that opens (**Figure 8.30**).
18. Rename your document to *Wildlife story* and tap *Rename* (**Figure 8.31**).
19. Since you can't work in Photoshop and Fresco at the same time, you need to close this document by returning to the Photoshop Home screen. To do this, tap the Home icon 🏠 shown in **Figure 8.32**.

Figure 8.30 Rename

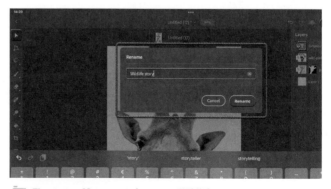

Figure 8.31 Name your document Wildlife story.

Figure 8.32 Close the document by returning to the Home screen.

Painting in Adobe Fresco

Now that the document is saved in Photoshop, we can take a trip to *Adobe Fresco* (**Figure 8.33**). As you read on page 5, Fresco is an app that lets you draw, paint and much more. Even if you don't have a Fresco premium subscription, you can do almost anything with it. Simply download Adobe Fresco from the App Store, log in with your Adobe ID and then start drawing and painting in Fresco in your Photoshop files or in a new document. You'll notice that the interfaces of Fresco and Photoshop are very similar. I think you'll quickly find your way around. Again, this is a Photoshop book, so I don't cover Fresco very extensively. But, I think it's just enough to introduce you to some of the best features. The combination of all apps makes your setup really powerful.

Figure 8.33 Painting in Adobe Fresco

1. Open *Adobe Fresco*. In the Fresco Home screen, you probably already see your Photoshop document. Tap the document thumbnail to open it. Don't see it? Then tap *Your Files* on the left side of the screen and select the document there (**Figure 8.34**).

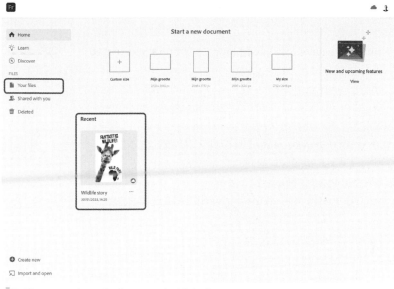

Figure 8.34 Open the document in Adobe Fresco.

2. Once you've opened the document, take a look around the
interface: You'll see the Photoshop banner with all its layers in
the Compact Layers panel on the right side of the screen. On the
left, you'll see the tools panel (**Figure 8.35**).

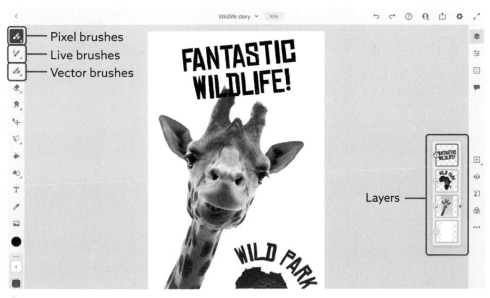

Figure 8.35 The Adobe Fresco Edit workspace

3. In the following steps, we'll draw a background color. To get ready, tap the bottom layer and then tap the + icon in the taskbar on the right side of the screen. A new layer will be added (**Figure 8.36**).

Now we're going to paint with a watercolor brush. These brushes work very true to life. You'll notice while painting that the paint even blends and runs as if it were real watercolor.

4. Tap the *Live Brushes* icon twice in the tools panel. The Watercolor and Oil brush categories appear. Choose *Watercolor* (**Figure 8.37**).
5. Choose *Watercolor Wash Soft* (**Figure 8.38**).
6. Then tap the *Color Picker* (**Figure 8.39**). I chose a light blue color, with *Hue* set at 200, *Saturation* at 20 and *Brightness* at 100.

Figure 8.36
New layer

Figure 8.37 *Watercolor*   Figure 8.38 *Choose a brush.*   Figure 8.39 *Choose a color.*

7. Let's make the brush nice and big. As in Photoshop, you can enlarge the brush by dragging up or down on the brush size number in the *Brush Settings* (**Figure 8.40**). Set the brush to a size of about *400 pixels*.

8. Paint a few individual brush strokes, letting them fade and blend like real watercolor paint. I think it looks best if the color is not completely even, but still a little smudgy (**Figure 8.40**).

Figure 8.40 Paint on the new layer.

We'll next add two more layers and paint on them with blue and green. The next steps are pretty much the same as the previous ones. Therefore, I'll describe them in a little less detail.

9. Create a new layer with the + icon in the taskbar on the right side of the screen (**Figure 8.41**).
10. If all is well, the same brush you used before is still selected. If not, select *Watercolor Wash Soft* again.
11. Change the color to darker blue. I chose *Hue* 191, *Saturation* 63 and *Brightness* 81 (**Figure 8.42**).
12. Reduce the brush size to about *180 pixels*.
13. Now draw with the blue brush behind the text (**Figure 8.43**).

Figure 8.41

New layer

Figure 8.42 Set the color.

Figure 8.43 Paint.

Figure 8.44 Set the color.

Figure 8.45 Paint.

14. Again, create a new layer with the + icon in the taskbar.
15. Change the color again. This time I chose *Hue* 126, *Saturation* 62 and *Brightness* 58 (**Figure 8.44**).
16. Set the brush size to about *420 pixels* and paint at the bottom of the banner (**Figure 8.45**).
17. Now save this document by tapping the file name at the top of the screen; then tap *Save Now*. Next, close the document and return to the Fresco Home screen using the arrow at the top left of the screen (**Figure 8.46**).

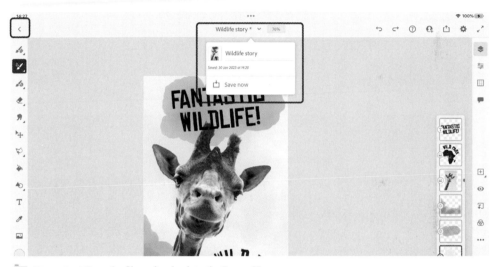

Figure 8.46 Save the file and go back to the Fresco Home screen.

Back to Photoshop

Now that we have finished painting in Fresco, we can continue working in Photoshop again. The updated file will automatically appear there. I recommend that you wait a moment before opening Photoshop. It may take a few seconds for the document to sync properly with Creative Cloud.

1. Open Photoshop. If all goes well, you should see the document in the Home screen (**Figure 8.47**). Don't see it? Then you can also take a look at *Your Files* on the left side of the screen.
2. Tap the document thumbnail. It'll open automatically.

Figure 8.47 Tap the document thumbnail to open the document.

Create a drop shadow

In the desktop version of Photoshop, you can create a drop shadow fairly quickly with Layer Effects. In Photoshop on the iPad, that feature is not yet present, but of course that doesn't mean you can't create a shadow. A little creativity and seeking adventure works wonders (remember Russell Brown's interview?), and another benefit is that with this exercise I can show you a few more things we haven't done before.

In the following steps we'll make the text white, then duplicate the text, make it black, turn that black text layer into a pixel layer, then blur the layer and make it transparent. Let's go!

1. Select the *Type* tool in the toolbar, and then tap the text on the canvas. You'll return to the Type workspace (**Figure 8.48**).

2. Tap the text once to get the context menu, then tap *Select All*.
3. Tap the Color Picker—next to *Color*—and change the color to white (**Figure 8.48**). Tap to close the Color Picker.

Figure 8.48 Recolor the text.

4. Tap *Done* when you're finished.
5. It's nicer if the text is behind the giraffe. Therefore, drag the layer down in the Layers panel until the text layer is just below the giraffe layer (**Figure 8.49**).
6. Duplicate the selected text layer by tapping the three dots at the bottom of the taskbar. Choose *Duplicate Layer* (**Figure 8.50**).

Figure 8.49 Select the layer.

Figure 8.50 Duplicate Layer

The layer is now duplicated (**Figure 8.51**). We'll make a shadow from this layer.

Figure 8.51 The duplicate layer

7. Select the *Type* tool in the toolbar and tap the text on the canvas.
8. You'll return in the Type workspace. Select the text by dragging over it, and change the color to black (**Figure 8.52**).

Figure 8.52 Change the color to black.

9. Tap *Done* when you're finished.

Before blurring the text with Gaussian Blur, you need to convert the layer to pixels. This is because you can't blur a text layer. Note that the layer will also be converted to pixels if you go to Gaussian Blur directly.

10. Go to the three dots at the bottom of the taskbar. Tap *Flatten Layer*. This will convert your layer to pixels (**Figure 8.53**).

11. Now tap the *Filters and Adjustments* button in the taskbar and choose *Gaussian Blur* (**Figure 8.54**).

Figure 8.53 Flatten Layer   Figure 8.54 Gaussian Blur

12. You enter the *Gaussian Blur* workspace. Set *Blur Amount* to about *2 or 3 pixels* (**Figure 8.55**).

Figure 8.55 Gaussian Blur workspace

13. Tap *Done* when you're finished.

14. Select the *Move* tool in the toolbar and move the shadow layer slightly downward at an angle. (**Figure 8.56**).

Figure 8.56 Move the shadow layer.

15. Now that the shadow is properly positioned, drag the layer below the white text in the Layers panel. This will ensure that the shadow is behind the text (**Figure 8.57**).

Figure 8.57 *Move the layer downwards.*

16. Finally, let's make the shadow slightly more transparent. Open the *Layer Properties panel*, if it's not already opened. Lower the *Opacity* to about *40%* (**Figure 8.58**).

Figure 8.58 *Lower the Opacity.*

Your social media image is ready to be posted! You can save it as a JPG or another file via the Export button at the top of the screen. (You can read how to do that on page 99.)

Of course, you can also return to the Home screen by tapping the arrow in the upper-left corner. Then you can continue working in Photoshop on the desktop if you wish. The Cloud Document is right there waiting for you on the Home screen. Clicking the document thumbnail opens the document. All your layers are editable there (**Figure 8.59**).

Figure 8.59 Continue in Photoshop on the desktop.

That's it for this exercise. Before I finish the book, I'll show you a few more options that we haven't covered yet. Other than that, I think all the different exercises have given you a good overview of the options in Photoshop on the iPad. I hope you enjoyed it. Keep experimenting and above all: Create lots of beautiful things!

Extra options

We've worked quite efficiently in this book. As a result, we were able to cover just about every option in Photoshop on the iPad in depth. I wrote at the beginning of this book that this is not a Photoshop on the iPad manual. It's a practical book that gives you a good overview of the capabilities of this fun program, and much more. I think that after going through the exercises, you'll also be capable of working with the program independently and discovering other features. Nevertheless, below I'll give you a brief overview of some features that weren't covered in the exercises. And, you'll read about new functions that will be added in the near future.

Photoshop App Settings

On the Photoshop Home screen, in the upper-right corner you'll see the icon of the account you are currently logged in with. When you tap that icon, the Photoshop app settings appear (**Figure 8.60**). These are settings that are usually already set properly, but are sometimes useful to review.

Figure 8.60 Photoshop App Settings

GENERAL: In this tab you'll find the Photoshop color theme settings. You can choose a dark (default) or light interface, or let Photoshop follow the iPadOS dark or light mode settings (**Figure 8.61**). If you prefer a light interface, you can choose that here. You can also reset the app settings by tapping *Restore App Defaults*.

INPUT: You can control the input of the Apple Pencil here (**Figure 8.62**). Do you find that the Apple Pencil responds too quickly when you tap the screen? Then increase *Pressure Sensitivity. Double Tap* lets you enable or disable a double tap on the flat side of the Apple Pencil, which, for example, lets you control the magnification of the canvas. You can also enable or disable various functions in the *Touch* section:

Touch Shortcut: Enable or disable the touch shortcut.

Stylus Only Painting: Only use the Apple Pencil or stylus for painting. If enabled, painting with your finger isn't possible.

Canvas Rotation: Enable or disable the ability to rotate your canvas.

Rotation Snapping: When you rotate the canvas in Photoshop, the rotation snaps to the horizontal and vertical positions. This is usually helpful, but if you prefer not to, you can turn it off here.

Show Touches: This is a useful feature when you record your screen and want to show your audience where you touch the screen with your stylus or finger. A blue circle will appear where you touch or tap the screen.

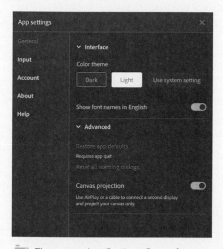

Figure 8.61 App Settings General

Figure 8.62 App Settings Input

ACCOUNT: Here you can manage your account settings, log in or out and see your remaining amount of Creative Cloud storage.

ABOUT: Information about Photoshop on the iPad.

HELP: Various links to help pages, tutorials and frequently asked questions. By the way, you can also find the same links if you tap the question mark found at the top-right corner of the screen when a document is open (**Figure 8.63**).

Figure 8.63 Photoshop Help

Brush settings

We have worked with brushes frequently in this book, but we didn't need the brush settings very often. Therefore, below you'll find a brief overview of the different brush settings.

BRUSHES PANEL: When you double-tap the Brush tool, you'll see a list of available brushes (**Figure 8.64**). When you open Photoshop for the first time, only the default brushes are available, but as you saw on page 106, you can also import other brushes.

BRUSH SETTINGS: You'll find the brush settings under the three dots in the Brush Settings menu (**Figure 8.65**). Here, as in Photoshop on the desktop, you can adjust the roundness, rotation angle, flow and smoothness of your brush. *Use Pressure for Size* sets the pressure sensitivity of your Apple Pencil. Soft pressure means a smaller brush; harder pressure means a larger brush. If you leave it disabled, the brush will always have the same size no matter how hard or soft you press. If you enable *Use Pressure for Opacity*, the brush will be more transparent if you press softly. If you press harder, the brush becomes less transparent.

Figure 8.64 Brushes

Figure 8.65 Brush Settings

MANAGE BRUSHES: If you want to manage your brushes or reset to the default brushes, you can tap the three dots at the top of the Brushes panel (**Figure 8.66**). Tap *Reset to Default Brushes* to reset. If you tap *Manage Brushes*, you can manage the brushes as shown in **Figure 8.67**. Tap a brush or brush group, and you'll be able to tap the three dots to delete or rename it. Tap the toggle to enable or disable the brush or brush group.

Figure 8.66 Manage Brushes

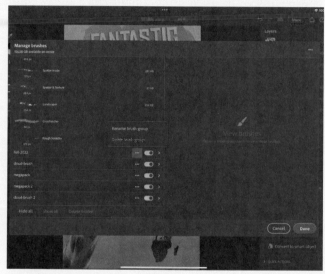

Figure 8.67 Deactivate or delete brushes.

The Eraser tool

About the Eraser we can be brief: You can erase pixels with it (**Figure 8.68**). It's a tool with almost the same settings as the Brush tool. You also have a choice of the same brushes and pressure sensitivity options. I actually never use the Eraser because I prefer to use layer masks to erase parts of a layer. The eraser works destructively; layer masks work non-destructively.

Figure 8.68 The Eraser tool

The Gradient tool

The *Gradient* tool can be found in the toolbar in the same tool group as the Paint Bucket tool (**Figure 8.69**). It allows you to create gradients by drawing a line in a certain direction (**Figure 8.70**). Photoshop uses the two colors you set as foreground color and background color (**Figure 8.70**). If you set the colors to light blue and dark blue, the gradient goes from light blue to dark blue (**Figure 8.71**).

Figure 8.69 Gradient tool

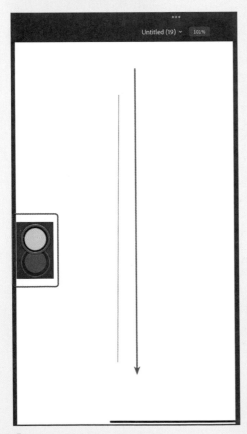

Figure 8.70 Draw a gradient.

Figure 8.71 The gradient

The Magic Wand tool

The *Magic Wand* is the oldest "smart" selection tool in Photoshop. I actually hardly ever use this tool anymore because I can usually make all the selections with the other, smarter tools, such as the Object Selection tool, the Quick Selection tool and Select Subject.

In certain cases the Magic Wand can be useful such as if you want to select areas of (almost) the same color.

With the Magic Wand you can tap an area containing more or less the same color. Photoshop will then try to select all adjacent areas of that color. In **Figure 8.72**, I tapped the dog's black fur and made a selection with the default Magic Wand settings.

If you set a higher *Tolerance* in the Magic Wand tool settings (**Figure 8.73**), more pixels will be selected because Photoshop is now looking at a wider range of colors. If you set the Tolerance to 255, everything in the layer will be selected; if you set Tolerance to 1, only the exact same color will be selected. As with all other selection tools, you can tap and hold the primary touch shortcut to add parts to the current selection.

Figure 8.72 Magic Wand (default) Tolerance 32

Figure 8.73 Magic Wand Tolerance 67

The Adjustment tools

Photoshop also has a number of *Adjustment tools* (**Figure 8.74**), which allow you to paint adjustments on an image, such as dark and light, saturation and less saturation and smudge pixels:

DODGE TOOL: The *Dodge* tool is a tool that allows you to paint highlights on an image. In the *Dodge Settings* (**Figure 8.75**), you can control which range is affected by this tool. By default, *Range* is set to *Midtones*, which causes the midtones to be lightened when you draw over an area in the image. If you select *Highlights*, the highlights you draw over will be made even lighter. The same applies to *Shadows*: The shadows you paint on will be lightened.

You can also set the brush size and the hardness of the Dodge tool. The *Exposure* setting is particularly interesting, because there you can control the degree of exposure—or speed—of the brush. The higher the Exposure, the faster the painted area gets lighter. If you lower the Exposure, your brush paints slower.

Figure 8.74 Adjustment tools

Figure 8.75 Dodge Settings

You can see a before and after example in **Figure 8.76** and **Figure 8.77**. I painted an extra sun beam with the Dodge tool.

BURN TOOL: The *Burn* tool works exactly the same as the Dodge tool, except that it darkens, rather than lightens, the areas you paint on. You can set the speed, hardness and size of the brush, as well as the range: midtones, highlights and shadows.

Figure 8.76 Before using the Dodge tool   Figure 8.77 After using the Dodge tool

SPONGE TOOL: The *Sponge* tool is a brush that can make colors less saturated or more saturated, depending on the *Sponge Settings* under *Mode* (**Figure 8.78**). If Mode is set to *Desaturate,* the colors become less intense, while *Saturate* makes the colors more intense. Again, this brush has options to set the size, hardness and speed (in this case called *Flow*). Usually the Sponge tool is used to make colors a little more intense in certain areas of a photo.

Figure 8.78 Sponge Settings

SMUDGE TOOL: The *Smudge* tool actually doesn't quite fit into the same category as the Dodge, Burn and Sponge tools. This is because it does nothing with color or light. It smudges away pixels. For example, you can use the Smudge tool to draw over edges that you want to soften a bit. We could have used the Smudge tool instead of Gaussian Blur when we softened the light of the lighthouse in Chapter 4. The Smudge tool gives a bit of the same effect as when you run your finger over paper that has just been painted on or drawn with charcoal.

Figure 8.79 and **Figure 8.80** show a before-and-after example of drawing with the Smudge tool. As with the other Adjustment tools, you can adjust the speed, hardness and size of the brush.

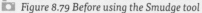 *Figure 8.79 Before using the Smudge tool*   *Figure 8.80 After using the Smudge tool*

The disadvantage of these tools is that you usually work directly on the pixels of the original photo. The tools are therefore less flexible, because you need to make a copy of your original layer to make sure you don't affect it, and it's more difficult to reverse actions afterwards.

Therefore, except for the *Smudge* tool, I always use adjustment layers with layer masks instead of these tools. For example, if you want to darken an image in certain areas, you can do this:

1. Add a clipped *Exposure* or *Curves* adjustment layer to the layer you want to darken.
2. Darken the image with the adjustment layer settings in the Properties panel.
3. Make the layer mask of that adjustment layer black: First select the layer mask in the Layers panel, then tap the lightning icon (*Filters and Adjustments*) in the taskbar and choose *Invert*. This will conceal everything in the adjustment layer.
4. Then paint with a white brush to reveal the adjustments and, if necessary, use a black brush to conceal any parts.

Instead of the Dodge and Burn tools you could use a Curves, Exposure or Levels adjustment layer, and instead of the Sponge tool you could use a Vibrance or Hue/Saturation adjustment layer.

The remaining adjustment layers

We used several adjustment layers in the exercises, like Curves and Hue/Saturation. With these two adjustment layers you can do almost anything you want. But, sometimes it can be useful to use one of the other adjustment layers. Here's an overview of the possibilities. Feel free to try them out on an image.

ADD ADJUSTMENT: You've seen this menu before (**Figure 8.81**). It opens when you tap the + icon in the taskbar and then Adjustment Layer, or when you tap Add Clipped Adjustment in the Properties panel.

BRIGHTNESS/CONTRAST: Two sliders with which you can very easily increase or decrease brightness and contrast (**Figure 8.82**). In the exercises, we did this with Curves because they provide more control.

Figure 8.81 Add Adjustment

Figure 8.82 Brightness/Contrast

BLACK AND WHITE: Converts the underlying layer or layers to black and white. Using the sliders you can determine which colors become lighter or darker (**Figure 8.83**).

COLOR BALANCE: Changes the color balance in the underlying layers or layers. Want more cyan in your image? Then move the Cyan/Red slider a little to the left (**Figure 8.84**). You could also do this with Curves, but Color Balance might be just a little faster and more intuitive to use.

EXPOSURE: Controls the amount of light in your picture. Slide Exposure to the left to make the picture darker and to the right to make it lighter (**Figure 8.85**). In the exercises we did this with Curves, but Exposure is sometimes just a little faster and more intuitive.

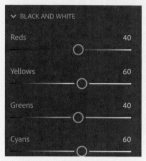

Figure 8.83 Black and White

Figure 8.84 Color Balance

Figure 8.85 Exposure

LEVELS: Controls how tonal levels are distributed from dark to light. This panel is does about the same as Curves, but is much more limited. (**Figure 8.86**).

VIBRANCE: Increases the intensity of the colors in your photo (**Figure 8.87**). Vibrance and Saturation are somewhat similar. The only difference is that Vibrance is a little smarter in that sense: If you increase Vibrance, saturation is increased more quickly for colors that are less intense. Colors that are already very intense are not adjusted as quickly. This reduces the chance of oversaturated colors. Increasing Saturation makes all colors more intense at the risk of oversaturation.

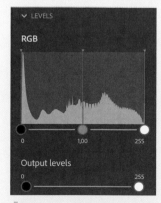

Figure 8.86 Levels

Figure 8.87 Vibrance

Photoshop on the iPad in the future

Wow, we've really covered almost all the features of Photoshop on the iPad now. Of course, the app continues to evolve. Once every few months a new update is released. Sometimes with a little more new features, other times with a little less. So it may well be that the app has already got some new features after you bought this book. That shouldn't be a big problem, because the basic features remain essentially the same. You'll see the new additions automatically in the Home screen and in the *New and Upcoming Features* section after there has been a new update. The Home screen already promises a number of things that will be added in the future. A brief overview:

SHARPEN YOUR IMAGE: A function that allows you to improve definition in image details. If you currently want to do this in Photoshop on the iPad, you can send the image to Lightroom for mobile, as we did in one of the exercises. Of course, you can also open and sharpen your image in Photoshop on the desktop.

GRIDS AND GUIDES: Rules that don't print or export and make it easier to align objects

COLOR SWATCHES: A panel where you can save and reuse your favorite colors.

LAYER EFFECTS: The Layer Effects also found in Photoshop on the desktop, which include *Drop Shadow*, *Outer Glow* and *Stroke*.

SHAPES: The ability to draw circles, rectangles and free forms as non-destructive vector (path-based) layers.

LIQUIFY: I'm really looking forward to this feature that is also present in Photoshop on the desktop and allows you to distort and warp objects more easily.

SMART FILTERS: Non-destructive filters, applied to Smart Objects. With Smart Filters, you can easily adjust filters such as Gaussian Blur and Liquify afterwards.

Chapter 9

Magdiel Lopez

ONE COLORFUL POSTER A DAY

Magdiel Lopez was born in Havana. There, at an early age, he was inspired by the colorful Cuban culture, which you can still find in his work today. When he was 15, he moved to Dallas in the United States. There he decided to design one poster a day and post it on his Instagram channel every day for 365 days. That ambitious idea caught the attention of media such as *The New York Times* and *Cosmopolitan*, gaining him more and more fame in the creative world. Magdiel currently works as a design mentor for Adobe. In Dallas, he runs his own creative agency and works with companies such as Apple, Nike and Warner Brothers. If you've seen the *Wonder Woman* movie posters, you've seen his work.

Name:	Magdiel Lopez
Residence:	Dallas, Texas, USA
Finds inspiration:	By coming up with cool concepts
Favorite tool:	Brushes
Most used tools:	Selections, masks and adjustment layers
Other favorites:	Adobe Fresco, Glitché and Over
Best advice:	Hang in there!

How do you work with Photoshop on the iPad?

A few years ago, I set myself a goal: I wanted to create an artistic poster every day in Photoshop under the title *A Poster a Day*. In those posters, I mix photos and paint with brushes. I usually come up with a concept and then create a series of posters around it. I still create such a poster almost every day and then post them on my Instagram channel. Some posters I created entirely in Photoshop on the iPad, the rest in a combination of iPad apps and Photoshop on the desktop.

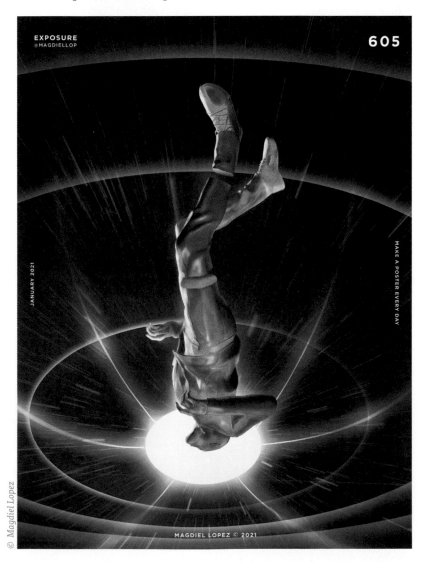

I think an iPad is much more inviting to experiment. The device works incredibly intuitively. I use brushes more often because painting on an iPad almost feels like I'm painting on paper. On a computer, I'm more limited in my options. As a result, I find posters I design on the iPad more instinctively artistic than those I create entirely on the computer.

How would you describe the style of your posters?

My posters are never hyper-realistic. Some artists create complete worlds in Photoshop with perfect lighting, colors and shadows. I like that, but I don't do it myself. I describe my work more as colorful, surrealistic and abstract. The feeling that my poster triggers something in people is more important to me than a perfect, realistic design.

Do you use the iPad often?

Nowadays, Photoshop on the iPad is a big part of my workflow. Sometimes I start a new document on the iPad, then continue in Photoshop on the desktop, then finish it again on the iPad. Switching back and forth between devices is very fast since documents are automatically synchronized via Creative Cloud. This way I get the best of both worlds: the intuitiveness of the iPad and the advanced capabilities of the desktop.

© Magdiel Lopez

© Magdiel Lopez

@MAGDIELLOP

@MAGDIELLOP

@MAGDIELLOP

By Magdiel Lopez

© Magdiel Lopez

What other iPad apps do you use in your design work?

I use *Adobe Fresco* a lot. This is mainly because Fresco has a very extensive brush set, with watercolor, oil, vector and pixel brushes. Switching between Fresco and Photoshop on the iPad is very quick because Photoshop documents automatically appear in the Fresco Home screen and vice versa. I also find the *Lasso tool* in Fresco easier to work with than in Photoshop on the iPad. In Fresco, you can use the Lasso to create straight and curved lines at the same time. This makes selecting and cutting out photos easier. The Lasso tool in Fresco reminds me a bit of the *Pen tool* I use a lot in Photoshop on the desktop.

© Magdiel Lopez

© Magdiel Lopez

In addition, I occasionally make use of *Glitché*. That's an app that lets you distort photos and add glitches. That causes a fun, unpredictable effect. Another app I often use is *Over*. When my poster is done, I save it in Photoshop and open that file in Over. I add a frame with the title of the poster there before I post it on Instagram.

What iPad are you currently working on?

An 11-inch iPad Pro with an Apple Pencil 2.

Which Photoshop artists are you inspired by?

That changes quite a bit. I'm constantly coming across new artists on social media. Currently I'm a fan of Elia Pellegrini, Doan Ly and Martyna Wędzicka-Obuchowicz (known as Wedzicka). All three of them have a very distinctive style. Elia

creates dreamy, atmospheric photo compositions, Doan Ly photographs still lifes of flowers, plants and models, and Wedzicka designs graphic objects with bright colors and flashy typography. I think you can find something of all three of these styles in my work.

Do you have any tips for people starting with Photoshop on the iPad for the first time?

Hang in there! Personally, I always tended to quickly go back to Photoshop on the desktop because I could already work so well with it. But, when my computer died and I was forced to work on the iPad for a while, I found that the iPad enriched my workflow. The things you can do with the Apple Pencil in combination with the touch screen you don't achieve as quickly on a computer. So always embrace the challenge of learning something new!

Index

C

Camera Raw Filter, 112
cameras
    iPad, 18, 185
    iPhone, 119, 123
    Lightroom for mobile, 123
    placing images from, 185
    transferring photos from, 10
canvas
    auto-selecting layers on, 30, 31
    rotating, 84, 85, 86, 205
Capture app, 4
Channels feature, 120
Chin, Ted, xii, xviii, 34–43, 46
Cihi, Frankie, xiii, xviii, 166–173
clipped adjustment layers, 27, 63, 94, 135
Clone Stamp tool, 142–146
Cloud Brush, 106–109
Cloud Documents, 3, 10, 12, 96, 98, 160
Color Balance adjustment layer, 213
color bar, 73
Color panel (Lightroom), 151
Color Picker, 194, 199
Color Swatches panel, 215
color theme settings, 204
color values, 73
Colorize option, 137
colors
    brush settings for, 72–73, 84, 87
    changing with Hue/Saturation, 94–95
    Color Picker for choosing, 194, 199
    filling selections with, 76
    Lightroom adjustments for, 114, 151
    removing from edges, 61
    Vibrance adjustments for, 214
Comments panel, 103
Compact layer view, 21, 29
compositions. See photo compositions
Content Aware Fill, 158–160
contrast
    Brightness/Contrast adjustment layer
    for, 213
    Curves adjustments for, 64–66, 136
    Lightroom adjustments for, 114, 151
copying exercise files, iv–v
Create New option, 17, 48
Creative Cloud
    file access, 3

subscription options, 2
Creative Cloud app, iv, 3, 10
    adding fonts through, 186–188
    renaming files in, 97
Creative Cloud Libraries
    creating new, 182–183
    placing files into Photoshop from,
    184–185
    uploading files to, 183–184
Crop & Rotate tool (Lightroom), 155
Crop and Rotate workspace, 131
Crop tool, 131
cropping images
    in Lightroom, 155
    in Photoshop, 131
Curves
    how they work, 64–66
    improving light with, 134–136
    nodes used in, 64, 66, 135–136
    vignette effect with, 138–139
Curves adjustment layer, 62–63, 66, 135–
    136, 138
Curves panel, 64, 65

D

Dali, Salvador, 42
Decontaminate Colors option, 61
Deleted files section, 17
deleting
    brushes, 207
    nodes from Curves, 64
    See also removing
Deselect button, 56, 159
Detail layer view, 21, 51
Detail panel (Lightroom), 151
Discover New Brushes option, 110
Discover section of Home screen, 17
Document Properties panel, 162
documents
    creating new, 17, 48
    exporting, 99–101
    naming/renaming, 96–97, 191
    Photoshop Cloud, 3, 10, 12, 96
    sizing/resizing, 162–163
    version history for, 104–105
    See also files
Dodge tool, 210, 211

H

hardness setting, 73, 84, 87
header bar, 19
Help feature
    gestures list, 32
    links related to, 205
    touch shortcuts list, 33
highlight adjustments, 64, 114, 136, 154
histogram, Curves panel, 64
Home screen, 16–18
    options list, 17–18
    renaming files in, 97
    returning to, 96
Hue slider, 95, 137
Hue/Saturation adjustment layer
    changing colors with, 94–95
    sepia effect using, 136–137
hues, color, 73, 95

I

Illustrator app, 5, 172
Image Size option, 162–163
images
    cropping, 131, 155
    editing raw, 147–161
    flipping, 80, 88
    placing into Photoshop, 49–52, 184–186
    repositioning, 53, 71
    retouching, 128–146
    rotating, 86, 131
    saving, 100
    scaling, 49, 53, 58, 91–92
    sharpening, 115, 151
    transforming, 49, 50
Import and Open option, 17–18, 130
importing
    additional brushes, 106–111
    photos as Smart Objects, 165
in-app subscription, 2
inspiration, sources of, 124
Instagram Story creation, 176
interface appearance options, 204
inverting selections, 138
inviting edits/reviews, 102–103
iPad

Apple Pencil used on, 6–8
apps recommended for, 2–5
camera used on, 18, 185
choosing your model of, 6–8, 11
editing between desktop and, 98
fonts added to, 186–188
Photoshop redesign for, xvi–xvii, 11
putting files on, 9–10
iPhone photography, 119, 123

J

Johansson, Erik, 42
JPG files, 99, 112, 123, 147

K

keyboard shortcuts, 12, 124
Knoll, Thomas and John, 117
Kush, Vladimir, 42

L

Lasso tool, 74, 75, 81–82, 158, 222
Layer Effects feature, 215
Layer Mask button, 28
layer masks
    creating, 56, 70, 181
    Curves, 138–139
    Decontaminate Colors, 61–62
    modifying, 83–86
    overview of, 28–29
Layer Properties panel, 22, 26–27, 51, 94,
    136, 202
layers, 24–31
    creating new, 72, 75, 87, 107, 132
    flattening, 201
    grouped, 31, 92–93
    masks on, 28–29
    moving, 30–31
    renaming, 72, 87
    reordering, 25, 71, 199
    selecting, 30–31, 92
    Smart Object, 165

T

taskbar, 21
text
    adding to documents, 188–191
    blurring, 200, 201
    color changes for, 199, 200
    downloading fonts for, 186–188
    drop shadow added to, 198–202
text layers, 199–200
Texture slider (Lightroom), 151
TIFF file format, 99
Tool Options panel, 22, 54, 81, 132
toolbar, 20
tools
    finding and activating, 20
    See also specific tools
touch shortcuts
    enabling and disabling, 204
    primary and secondary, 20, 33
    selection adjustments, 54, 55
Transform tool, 81, 86, 90, 190
Transform window, 49
Transform workspace, 81, 86
transformations
    flipping images, 80, 88
    rotating images and text, 86, 190
    scaling images, 49, 86
transparency
    adjusting, 52, 57, 74, 90, 202
    layer mask, 28, 70
    whites, 78
Type tool, 188, 198, 200
Type workspace, 188, 198–199, 200

U

Undo gesture, 32
Unsplash.com website, 5, 42
uploading files, 183
USB hub connection, 9
USB-C connection, 9

V

vector files, 184
version history, 104–105
Vibrance adjustment layer, 214
View at 100gesture, 32
vignette effect, 114, 137–141
Von Wong, Benjamin, 42

W

Webster, Kyle, 106, 110–111
Wędzicka-Obuchowicz, Martyna, 223
whites
    adjusting, 66, 150
    making transparent, 78
workspaces
    Crop and Rotate, 131
    Edit, 18–23, 96
    Gaussian Blur, 140
    Masking, 152
    raw-editing, 164, 165
    Refine Edge, 179–180
    Transform, 81, 86
    Type, 188

Y

Your Files section, 17

Z

zooming in/out, 32, 84